Authentic:
Dare to Be Real

———⚬⚬⚬———

Taffi Dollar

Scripture quotations marked (KJV) are taken from the *King James Version* of the Bible.

Scripture quotations marked (NKJV) are taken from *The New King James Version*, copyright © 1979, 1980, 1982 by Thomas Nelson, Inc.

Scripture quotations marked (AMP) are taken from *The Amplified Bible, Old Testament*, copyright © 1965, 1987 by The Zondervan Corporation. The Amplified New Testament, copyright © 1958, 1987 by the Lockman Foundation. Used by permission.

Scripture quotations marked (NIV) are taken from *The Holy Bible: New International Version®* NIV® copyright © 1973, 1978, 1984 by International Bible Society. Used by permission of Zondervan Publishing House. All rights reserved.

Scripture quotations marked (MSG) are taken from *The Message: New Testament with Psalms and Proverbs*, copyright © 1993, 1994, 1995 by Eugene H. Peterson, published by NavPress, P.O. Box 35001, Colorado Springs, Colorado 80935. Used by permission.

Scripture quotations marked (NLT) are taken from the *Holy Bible: New Living Translation*, copyright © 1996. Used by permission of Tyndale House Publishers, Inc., Wheaton, IL 60189. All rights reserved.

Webster's New World College Dictionary, 3rd Ed. New York: Simon & Schuster, Inc., 1996.

I would like to acknowledge the editorial services provided by Yolanda Harris in association with VisionWorks. Thank you for your assistance and flexibility on this project.

13 12 11 10   10 9 8 7 6 5 4 3 2 1

Authentic: Dare to Be Real
ISBN 13: 978-1-57794-933-6
ISBN 10: 1-57794-933-1

Published by Harrison House, Inc.
P.O. Box 35035
Tulsa, Oklahoma 74153
harrisonhouse.com

Then God said, "Let us make human beings in our image, to be like us."

Genesis 1:26 NLT

CONTENTS

INTRODUCTION

In 1968 Marvin Gaye and Tammi Terrell sang the hit song "Ain't Nothing Like the Real Thing." Although the song is not as popular as it once was, its title still rings true today. Whether we're talking about the latest designer clothes, a work of art, or even true love, we want the original or the real thing. The same concept can be compared to our personal lives.

Living an authentic lifestyle gives us the freedom, boldness, and tenacity to live life to the fullest—without apology. We are at liberty to be the best that we can be in every area of life because we are striving to live better, think better, and feel better about ourselves and others.

Being real means being authentic—daring to make your mark in the world without excuses and without fear. As true and genuine individuals, we are able to bring light into the darkness of deception, eliminating confusion and causing enlightenment. Living an authentic lifestyle enables us to be honest, transparent, and genuine individuals,who will positively impact and change the world around us.

I wrote this book so that others will discover their true purpose, giftedness, and uniqueness in life. Being true to who we really are will lead us to our true purpose and our real destiny. For many of us, living with true purpose means making adjustments and embracing change. I know I had to. But taking life a day at a time allows us to continuously strive to be our best as we trust our decision to keep pressing forward and trusting God. Making adjustments can be challenging, and they may take some time, but the results are truly worth it. Living each day with the ability to trust and believe in being ourselves is authentic living.

As you read these pages, I hope the message will linger in your heart as you discover and uncover the real you. You will find that the more you learn about you, the closer you will come to the authentic masterpiece you have been created to be—the "you" the world is in expectation to see. So, arise and take your place. Dare to be authentic. Dare to be real. Dare to be you.

Chapter 1

I AM WHO I AM

There is a popular soda commercial that contains the slogan, "Image is nothing; thirst is everything." While this is a catchy saying, I believe image is everything, particularly the image we have of ourselves. Everywhere we turn, we are bombarded with images of what manhood and womanhood should be according to the standards of society. The news media, sitcoms, magazines, movies, and many other forms of published material are intended to shape the way we see ourselves. However, most of those images are not accurate reflections of who we really are, nor do they paint a clear picture of why we were created.

To be *authentic* is "to be real," "to be certified," and "to be proven." It is "verifiable evidence of what someone or something really is." To try to model our lives after the images we see around us will not bring out our authenticity as individuals but will, instead, cause us to conform to something other than who we are. How we see ourselves means everything, and, quite honestly, how we present ourselves to others can determine our achievement.

We all struggle with the image question, especially since we live in a world in which we are defined more so by what is on the outside than what is going on within. For ladies, the "superwoman" ideal is on the rise, which puts more and more pressure on women of all ages and backgrounds to be everything to everyone all the time while trying to live up to sometimes impossible standards. Men aren't exempt either. They are told their successes are determined by the dollar amount in their bank accounts rather than the integrity of their character. Sadly, too many people become victims of the pressures of the world, and they end up becoming burned-out spiritually, emotionally, and physically.

There was a time in my life when I really had concerns about what others thought of me. This fear negatively affected my confidence in myself and my abilities. For example, when it came to speaking in front of people, I was extremely uncomfortable. There were times when I told my husband, Creflo, I absolutely would not get up to preach in church; I would leave that to him! I was much more comfortable taking a background role. But I later discovered my purpose included speaking to large crowds. I then had to realize that in order to fulfill God's plan and purpose for my life, I had to change the way I saw myself. I had to see myself as God sees me.

When we don't know who we are and why we were put here, we can easily become wrapped up in someone else's definitions, which can be dangerous to our self-esteem. With this in mind, what is the image we should adapt as our personal reality? How can we create a new frame of identity reference for ourselves—one that allows us to embrace our uniqueness? I believe the answer is simple: trace self-image back to its source. We were all created for a distinct purpose; and as individuals, we have gifts, talents, and abilities that enable us to carve out a place for ourselves in this world without sacrificing our authenticity. We can be all we were created to be by simply understanding who we are.

CREATED IN GOD'S IMAGE

When you think of an image, what comes to your mind? I think of a picture of something. Images are always flashing before our eyes, eventually giving birth to the things we see on the screens of our minds. An *image* is a mental picture or vision of something. It is a reflection as well as a representation. It is a likeness of what is being reflected. For example, when you look in the mirror, you see an image of yourself reflected back at you. It is that image that gives you a clear picture of what you look like. Mirrors don't lie; what you see is what you get!

Just like we have a physical image we can see, there is also an inner image we cannot see. This is where our connection to God comes in. Discovering the starting point of our true image will trace us back to the mind of God who created every person in His image. This is essential to understanding our identity.

When I talk about God creating us in His image, I want you to think about how a child possesses some of the features and characteristics of his or her parents. The child may even have distinct mannerisms that clearly take after those of his or her parents. Children bear the likeness of their parents because they are their *offspring*. They carry their attributes. Well, this is how we can look at ourselves in relation to God.

First, God is a spiritual being, and when we say we are made in His image, it simply means we are also spiritual beings. You are a spirit; you possess a soul (the mind, will, and emotions); and you live in a physical body. This is the three-fold nature of every person. We are primarily like God because of the spiritual part of us, which is the very core of who we are. What also makes us like Him is the fact that we can speak life-giving words, and we have authority on the earth. This puts us in a tremendously powerful position as individuals because it means we are not subject to all the negative things that may be going on around us. We have the power to speak words that can change our situations and circumstances.

Before we were born, the Creator had an image of each one of us on the inside of Him. It was that visual picture I mentioned earlier. And that image contained not only our identity as representations of Him, but it also contained the particular purpose He designed for our lives. Contained within that purpose are all the gifts, talents, abilities, and passions that distinguish us as individuals.

We have to begin to see ourselves as God sees us. If we view ourselves as incompetent, inferior, or unqualified, we will never get far in life. For women, if we embrace the idea that our worth lies solely in our physical attributes, as the media suggests, then we will spend our lives seeking approval and recognition based on how we look on the outside. Men can also become consumed with fulfilling a distorted ideal of manhood that is rooted primarily in material possessions. However, when our worth comes from within, and when our inner image is one of success and victory based on God *in* us; this will eventually translate to every area of our lives. Nothing will be able to hold us back.

How we see ourselves makes all the difference in whether we are successful in life. Our inner image is so important. I began to understand that, many times, the way I saw myself determined how I was able to handle and overcome situations in my own personal life. It really took me making a decision to see a better image of myself to realize that I truly can do all things through Christ because He has given me the ability to do so. In order to conquer the fear that forced me to cling to the background, I had to embrace the image God had of me and become willing to see myself equipped by God to accomplish all He has created me to do.

The world has definitely grasped the concept of maximizing the inner image. It is everywhere! From popular talk-show hosts to people who have built multi-million-dollar businesses, people all over the world are visualizing their greatness and the potential inside of them. Many of these individuals do not have a personal relationship with God, and yet they have harnessed the power of having an inner image of success. Why should you be any different?

WORDS PRODUCE IMAGES

A conversation about images is not complete without dealing with the power of words, which plays a critical role in shaping our mindsets. Words are the creative force we can use to change and rearrange things in our lives. And the words we speak about ourselves, along with the words we receive from other people, make a big difference.

Creflo and I have encountered and counseled countless people who have been burdened and broken by the cares and pressures of life. There are many whose spirits and sense of self-worth have been crushed by verbal, emotional, and physical abuse. Some feel hopeless and helpless as they wrestle with personal inner struggles. What I've realized is that words are the starting point of negative emotions and low self-esteem, just as they are the stimulus for self-confidence and positive outcomes.

Have you ever experienced someone saying something negative to or about you that affected you long after it was spoken? This is because words are like containers which go down deep into a person's heart and soul. They have the potential to do great damage or good to the listener. For example, if you grew up with a parent who constantly told you how bad you were or that you wouldn't amount to anything, you most likely internalized those words and they began to shape your self-image. As the mother of three teenage girls, I have realized how important it is that I build their self-esteem by speaking positive words and affirmations into their spirits and their lives instead of negative ones.

Just as the effect of negative words can be tremendous, the results of speaking positive words can have a huge impact on shaping our lives as well. A word is like a seed that we plant in a garden. When that word goes into the soil of our hearts, it will eventually grow up to produce a harvest. The harvest of a positive self-image is the result of speaking positive words.

Too often we measure ourselves by what others have to say about us. However, we need to ask ourselves: what does God have to say about me? I like to use the illustration of a shy little girl, who is not exactly the most beautiful child in the world by the opinion of some. But if she is told over and over again that she is pretty, talented, and special, she will see herself that way. No matter what she sees out in the world, if her self-image is built up through positive words and affirmations on a daily basis, she will be confident in herself and the unique things that make her beautiful.

On the other hand, if that same little girl is told she is ugly, hopeless, or other negative things, what do you think will happen? She will adopt a poor self-image. She will most likely feel inferior, unworthy, and unattractive. And that inner image will draw negative people and experiences into her life.

Proverbs 18:21 contains timeless wisdom on the power of words: death and life are in the power of the tongue. Simply put, this means our words drive our lives in either a positive or negative direction; they shape our destinies. And it is usually the words that were spoken over our lives that we tend to repeat to ourselves.

Are you dealing with a wounded spirit? Have past words spoken over your life caused you to have low self-esteem or a negative self-image? If so, God's healing is available through speaking what *He* says over your life rather than replaying those old dialogues. You can create a healthy self-image through your words.

Every day is a new opportunity for you to build an inner image of success. You don't have to create an image for yourself because God has already done it for you! From the beginning, He has held a distinct image of each one of us in His mind. When you get up in the morning and look in the mirror, say something good about yourself. God already has. Think about your strengths rather than your weaknesses and shortcomings. Focus on the things that make you authentically you, and embrace the divine part of yourself that is a reflection of God!

BECOMING MORE LIKE HIM

I believe the objective of a successful life should be to go from level to level by constantly experiencing growth and development. Developing the right image on the inside of us is a process like anything else. There is always room for increase and improvement.

Personally, I can attest to the fact that it takes time to grow from having a self-image that is negative to one that is positive. I know what it feels like to have insecurities and fears that can paralyze you. But the Word of God is what makes the difference. One scripture that really speaks to me is 2 Corinthians 3:18 KJV: "But we all, with open face beholding as in a glass the glory of the Lord, are changed into the same image from glory to glory, even as by the Spirit of the Lord."

In other words, the Word of God is like a mirror that we look at to show us the reflection of who we really are. And if we gaze into the mirror of God's Word long enough and receive the images of peace, joy, faith, love, prosperity, wholeness, soundness, and healing reflected back at us, we will eventually find ourselves becoming more and more aware of these realities rather than the negative aspects of life. Ultimately, we will be completely transformed into that image!

Initially, when we look in a mirror, we tend to see the imperfections; they are the first things to jump out at us. They help us to notice the things that need to be changed or adjusted. Well, I believe the same thing is true when we first look into the mirror of God's Word. It can be difficult at first when all we see are our personal shortcomings and weaknesses. I'm talking about the fears, inadequacies, selfishness, and deeply-rooted negative self-images that have been ingrained in us over time. But we should not walk away from or even avoid the mirror just because we become aware of the places that need work. This process of conforming to the image of God in us is ongoing, and it will begin to affect our lives when we make a decision to see it through.

God is love; and because He is love, we are created in the image of love. I want you to think about this every time you are tempted to beat up on yourself or focus on the negative things someone has said about you. The real you is a person of love who possesses the very nature of God on the inside. Not only that, but God loves you just the way you are. He loves everything about you, from head to toe, because you came from Him. I don't know about you, but that excites me to no end! When you understand the reality that God loves you, you can then love yourself. Reminding yourself of this love gives you the ability to realize how special you are and the power and ability to love others. Because you were made in His image, you are worthy of love, positive relationships, and success. You are qualified to receive the very best.

PREDESTINED FOR A PURPOSE

God made you in His image for a reason, and there is a specific purpose for you in life. Think about your various strengths and abilities. Consider your personality traits and the things you are passionate about. These things are all a part of the assignment for your life, which is ultimately designed to touch others with the love and life of God. Combined with a consciousness of being made in His image, you become an unstoppable force in the earth; someone who can accomplish *anything* you set out to do.

I encourage you to examine the mindsets that hinder the development of a healthy self-image, such as feelings of low self-esteem, speaking the wrong words about yourself, being overly concerned with others' opinions of you, and trying to conform to worldly images of who you should be. All of these are obstacles to healthy emotional and spiritual development. Instead, concentrate on building the right image on the inside. This may mean separating from people who are not helping you to grow, even family members. It most definitely means becoming more conscious of what you say about yourself and of making positive declarations *on purpose*.

Our genuine image and purpose are wrapped up in something much greater than what we see in popular culture. It is the worth, treasure, and esteem that only come from God. It is love, peace, and wholeness. It is the true essence of authenticity, and it is inside of you!

To be *authentic* is "to be real," "to be certified," and "to be proven." It is "verifiable evidence of what someone or something really is." To try to model our lives after the images we see around us will not bring out our authenticity as individuals but will, instead, cause us to conform to something other than who we are.

- *We must have the proper self-image in order to be authentic people.*

Have you allowed your self-image to be defined by society?

_____

_____

Just as a child resembles his or her parents, in what ways do you resemble your heavenly Father?

_____

_____

_____

- *How we see ourselves makes all the difference in whether we are successful in life.*

Do you see yourself as victorious or defeated? Explain your answer.

_____

_____

_____

_____

• *Our self-image and mindsets are determined by words.*

Have you allowed the words of others to influence your self-image?

_____

_____

What positive words can you speak about yourself to make a difference in your self-image?

_____

_____

_____

What can you do to prevent the negative words of others from affecting your self-image?

_____

_____

_____

- *The objective of a successful life should be to go from level to level, and constantly experience growth and development.*

The Word of God is the mirror that shows us the reflection of who we really are. What would you like to change about your self-image, and how much time are you willing to spend reading the Word daily in order to make that change?

_____

_____

_____

_____

What are some mindsets that hinder you from having a healthy self-image?

_____

_____

_____

_____

When you understand the reality that God loves you, you can then love yourself. Write down several reasons why you know beyond a doubt that God loves you.

_____

_____

_____

_____

• *You were predestined for a specific purpose.*

To understand your purpose, consider your personality traits and write down the things you are most passionate about.

_____

_____

_____

_____

_____

What and who have shaped your self-image? Identify specific mindsets that have hindered or enhanced your ability to see yourself as God created you.

_____

_____

_____

_____

_____

Chapter 2

AUTHENTIC ATTITUDE

As we go through life, it is important that we choose our area of focus. Choosing a positive approach keeps us connected to the authentic lifeline of hope God has placed in each of us. In some instances, we focus on our circumstances, our current relationship status, health concerns, or financial situation. For example, if the doctor gives us a less-than-favorable diagnosis, we may worry and begin placing more focus on the news we received rather than the truth found in God's Word. God says that you are healed! So when the doctor's report differs from the authentic report God has given us, we have to choose to focus on God's Word. Even through the most tedious moments in life, we have to muster up the courage to activate our faith by believing His Word. Focusing on positive solutions and possible alternatives during difficult times helps us to maintain a positive outlook on life even when circumstances seem hopeless. By exercising our faith, we stretch and position ourselves to experience the miracles God has in store for us.

Some circumstances that occur in our lives have a way of dimming the positive aspects in our lives. It's not that positive things don't exist after negative situations have occurred; rather, it is the shift in our thinking that causes us to give more attention to that which is negative and less to that which is positive. As a result, the positive can rarely be seen and enjoyed. It is like the old cliché: we can't see the forest for the trees.

Staying positive in a negative world is not easy, but it can be done. In fact, it must be done if we want our faith to continually increase. To live a positive life, we must intentionally focus our attention on good things. The Bible urges us to fix our thoughts on things that are true and of a good report. God never asked us to focus on the economy, our bank accounts, or other challenges we face. He knows those things will discourage us and cause us to cave-in and quit.

Your bank account balance may not be where you need it to be right now. Your job security may seem a bit shaky, and your marriage may not be as fulfilling as you desire. But it doesn't help to focus on the negative aspects of your situation. These things are temporal, which means they are subject to change. Instead, thank God that you have a bank account, job, or marriage. Seek Him for the answers you need, and allow Him to direct your path. The key to having a positive outlook on life is to focus more on God and less on the challenges you face. He is the only One who can sustain you while you're going through and bring you out better than you were before.

There are times when focusing on the positive is a lot harder to accomplish than those around us might imagine. Very few people know the impact negative situations can sometimes have in our lives. And every now and then they may tell us to "get over it!" While getting over it is what we *want* to do, it is much easier said than done. Sometimes life shocks us in such a way that it leaves us completely numb. I've been there. When my mother went home to be with the Lord, I simply wasn't prepared. I didn't see it coming, but even if I had, dealing with her absence in my life would not have been any less painful.

You, too, may have experienced some form of loss: the death of a loved one, divorce, or a job layoff. Perhaps you're dealing with a setback related to a relationship, health, or finances. There are people who struggle with deeply-rooted issues that sometimes lead to feelings of low self-esteem and hopelessness. Unforgettable events such as physical, verbal, and mental abuse, abortion, alcoholism, drug addiction, prostitution, and even incarceration can be overwhelming. The truth of the matter is that despite the origin of the negative or unjust circumstances you encounter, God is always with you. In Him alone you can find the strength to grow and the courage to move forward.

Maybe none of these examples quite fit your current or past circumstances, but chances are you know someone in your family, community, or workplace who is dealing with one of these or similar situations. Although you may not be completely aware of the challenges the person is enduring, your positive attitude can have a tremendous impact on their recovery. Just as we want others to be sensitive toward us, we must also be sensitive to them. We may never know why a person thinks or behaves the way he or she does, but we can be a positive force in their lives by demonstrating love, compassion, and respect.

LIFE ISN'T ALWAYS FAIR

Circumstances are a part of life. Jesus said: "In this world you will have trouble. But take heart! I have overcome the world" (John 16:33 NIV). No matter how much money we have, the position we hold, the title we carry, or how holy we may be, we cannot escape the troubles associated with life. Sometimes things just don't work out like we plan. For example, a person may choose a partner and get married for better or worse. Someone else may choose a friend and believe that that person will always be there for them. Another person may start a new job or launch a new business and expect great success. Yet despite high hopes and exceptional planning, there are times when the things we invest our hopes, trust, and finances in fail us without warning.

The good news is that the Creator has established a prearranged plan for the challenges we will encounter in life. Our job is to trust Him, no matter how difficult things may seem. Naturally, the human tendency is to react by fighting back, getting even, or just giving up. But unfortunately, reacting doesn't solve the problem. Responding is a better option.

RESPONDING VS. REACTING

Sometimes the biggest challenge in dealing with our problems is understanding what to do and how we should respond. To find the answers, we must seek God and His perspective on our situations. This is not the time to run away from God because we fear that He will be disappointed in us. He understands that we will make mistakes along the way, and He promises never to condemn or turn His back on us. He is always there, ready to guide us to the next step in our lives.

When circumstances in our lives cause us discouragement or worry, we have to make a choice. Either we're going to let it get the best of us by giving all our attention to it for the next few days, months, or years; or we're going to respond rather than choose to react. When we choose to respond, we give the steering wheel to God and take the backseat. I say the backseat because too often we take the passenger seat and are tempted to copilot. God doesn't need our help to navigate through the storm; He is more than able to handle it. Remember, God already knows the end from the beginning.

Once we give God the wheel, we have to trust Him. For example, let's say you were planning a road trip that you have never taken before. Your brother, on the other hand, is very familiar with the drive because he has traveled it many times. In a case like this, it would be in your best interest to let *him* navigate the trip. Through his experiences, he has learned all the detours to take to avoid traffic and construction and is, therefore, the best person for the job. But if you sit in the passenger's seat with an open map to copilot and you begin questioning his judgment and telling him what the map says he should do, you're going to frustrate him. Eventually he will stop the car and let you drive. Then you'll be in the same position you were in at the beginning—navigating the trip alone and needlessly exhausted by the experience. Had you allowed your brother to drive and rested in his ability to do so, you would have arrived at your destination sooner, feeling refreshed and energized.

This is a good example of how we treat God sometimes. We ask Him to get involved in our situations; then, we begin telling Him what we want Him to do and how we want Him to do it. In our minds, we know just how the problem should be resolved. When God's plan appears to be different from our own, we are tempted to take over the wheel. As a result, we become frustrated and disappointed with the outcome. Sometimes, without even realizing we have taken the wheel again, we blame God for the things that could have been avoided had we given Him complete control.

To respond appropriately to life's troubles, our first decision is to surrender our concerns to God *and leave them there!* Notice I used the word *respond.* As I said before, responding and reacting are two different things. When things happen to us, it is natural to react. Reacting may involve emotions like crying, getting angry, or taking revenge. It is okay to cry or get angry but then release it. Don't seek revenge. Take control of the situation. God has given us the authority to speak life into our circumstances when we react with the faith we possess as an overcomer. Even though He has given us emotions, it is not His will that they control our lives. When we stay in reaction mode, it leads to trouble. That's when bitterness, envy, depression, and self pity set in. It is virtually impossible to have a positive attitude when these feelings overtake us.

Don't let emotions fester for long periods of time. Let them go, release your faith, and start saying things like, "I know I'm coming out of this situation. This is a test that I am well able to pass. No matter what it looks like or how I feel, I trust God. He will never leave me or forsake me!" Before you know it, your situation will start to turn around.

The second response is to allow God to guide us through the difficult times. Being in constant prayer about the situation and reading the Word will give us the peace and direction we so desperately need. They help us to remain positive when everything inside of us wants to focus on the negative. Many would be surprised by how their perspectives about the situation can change when they get God involved. There is no point in overreacting, questioning God, or feeling sorry for yourself. Reacting is never the best solution.

DON'T BE MOVED BY WHAT YOU SEE

Psalm 34:19 NIV says, "A righteous man may have many troubles, but the LORD delivers him from them all." Everyone is going to encounter problems in life, even the person who is in right standing with God. We can expect it because He said so. However, the last part of this Scripture assures us that when the time comes, God will be there to rescue us. Not only *will* God deliver us, He *wants* to deliver us.

Some people stop going to church when bad things happen to them. They mistakenly believe that they are unworthy of God's blessings and forgiveness. Others stay away because they fear other Christians will shun them or talk about their private issues publicly. Then there are those who want to come to church and accept Christ as their Savior, but they feel inadequate or ashamed. Sadly, they believe they have to fix all their problems *before* giving their lives to Him. They are convinced that once they get themselves together, it will be okay to join the church and get saved. The truth of the matter is we can't fix our problems. Apart from God, there is just no way! We need Him to deliver us. Therefore, when troubles come, we must invite Him in. He's a gentleman. God is never going to force His way into our situations. He wants us to want Him there.

The state of the economy has played a significant role in the lives of many people over the past few years. In fact, I can't imagine that there is anyone in America who has not experienced some impact from the economic crisis. People have lost their jobs and homes, and some have diminished or completely emptied their life's savings. Just watching the news can trigger hopelessness. Even though the reality is that the economy has affected our lives, dwelling on it won't change the situation. We can't be moved by things we see like high gas prices, closing businesses, and negative bank balances. Our focus should be on the One who can change it all.

There is a lot of darkness in the world now. And if the only thing we're feeding off of is negative television, negative news reports, and negative people, we're going to be negative. Thank God there are positive options also available through television, radio, music, books, and even magazines. When we take in negative information, we are influenced by it and ultimately participate in it by complaining and finding fault in others.

I am reminded of the story of Caleb in Numbers 13 and 14. Moses and the Israelites were traveling through the desert in search of the Promised Land. God told Moses that Canaan was the place designated for His people to inhabit. He asked Moses to send spies to inspect the land and its people. The land was already rich in resources and filled with everything they could possibly want or need.

When the twelve spies returned, they confirmed that the land was indeed flowing with milk and honey. The grapes were sweet and ripe, and everything was plentiful. But soon their report became flooded with doom and gloom about the people who lived there. All they could focus on was how big the people were. As a result, the spies feared they would be destroyed. They described the people in Canaan as giants! Rather than seeing themselves equipped for potential battle, the spies described themselves, and their own people as small, defeated grasshoppers. The Israelites heard the report and began to stir. They constantly complained and were overcome by fear.

However, Caleb, one of the spies, had a different report. He saw the same land and the same people the other spies saw, but he chose to see things from a positive perspective. Here is his account:

Caleb interrupted, called for silence before Moses and said, "Let's go up and take the land—now. We can do it." But the others said, "We can't attack those people; they're way stronger than we are." They spread scary rumors among the People of Israel. They said, "We scouted out the land from one end to the other—it's a land that swallows people whole. Everybody we saw was huge. Why, we even saw the Nephilim giants …. Alongside them we felt like grasshoppers. And they looked down on us as if we were grasshoppers."

Numbers 13:30-33 MSG

Even after hearing Caleb's report, the people were overcome with fear and began complaining to and about Moses. Rather than accepting the hope Caleb's report provided, they chose to believe the negative report of the other spies. Once again, they thought that God had abandoned them. The same God who saved them from the Egyptians by parting the Red Sea, freed them from slavery, and sustained them while in the desert was about to fulfill the promise He had made to them to possess their own land. Yet they doubted Him and began to wish that they were still enslaved in Egypt.

The Israelites were relentless. They began to rebel against God, planned to fire Moses and Aaron, and plotted to kill Caleb and Joshua. God was absolutely furious with them. Initially, He planned to kill the Israelites, but Moses pleaded for God's mercy. Wow! There they were, secretly trying to get rid of Moses, and there he was, pleading to God to spare their lives. Some trade off. God honored Moses' request, and rather than destroying them, He extended their journey for forty long years. (*I encourage you to read the story; there's a whole lot more!*) God was not so merciful to the ten spies who incited fear and rebellion among the people: they were struck dead.

However, God spared the lives of Caleb and Joshua. If only the Israelites had believed Caleb's report, they could have possessed the land almost immediately. That was God's plan.

How many blessings have we missed out on by choosing to focus on the negative? I believe one of the most valuable lessons we can learn from this story is the value of choosing a positive perspective. Had the Israelites chosen to believe Caleb's report, they would have entered into the Promised Land in God's timing. Instead, they opted to believe all the negative things they heard, and as a result, they were overtaken with fear.

The perspective by which we view our circumstances generally determines the type of life we will lead and the results we will achieve. The results the Israelites received would have been far better had they chosen to trust Caleb's optimistic perspective. Instead, they bought into the negative report, complained, and remained ungrateful. Canaan flowed with milk and honey just as God said. The spies confirmed that it was filled with everything they could ever need or desire. Sure there were giants, but as Caleb reminded them, God was on their side. Their victory was guaranteed!

Being positive is a choice. We can choose to see the glass as half full, or we can choose to see it as half empty. Either way, it's the same glass. Caleb, as well as Joshua, saw the glass half full while the other ten spies saw it as half empty. These great men of faith were able to see beyond the obstacles and embrace the destiny God had prepared for them. Although they were outnumbered, it was Caleb and Joshua's optimistic view that earned God's favor. He blessed them by allowing them and their descendants to live in the land.

GOD'S AUTHENTIC NATURE REVEALED

When we respond to life's obstacles with great faith and determination, we reflect the true and authentic nature of God. It is generally in the darkest times that light is seen. Think about it. When the power goes out in your home and you light a small match, it illuminates the place. Think what would happen if each of us allowed our small light to shine in the world. We would eventually overtake darkness and evil.

It is during difficult times that God's nature is best displayed and the magnificence of His love is revealed. In His Word, God encourages you to become like His Son, Jesus. To do so, you must constantly engage in the transformation process of renewing your mind. If you've been a person who sees the cup as half empty, it's time to change your perspective. Begin seeing your circumstances through an optimistic lens. The optimist sees the glass as half full, never half empty. Program your mind to believe that there is an assured victory on the other side of your situation. If you can see it, you can achieve it.

God has already placed the ability to achieve great things inside of you. He has also placed in you the ability to take on a positive stance in the midst of trouble. I think sometimes in life we become so overwhelmed by our emotions and the situations we face that we lose perspective of the hope found in the Bible. How we view the situation determines whether we will see God in it with us or see ourselves alone. With Him, we can do all things. When He gets involved, we can expect to overcome every situation and experience the better things He has in store for us.

Attitude determines altitude. Like a plane, when the nose is pointed upward, it soars and is less inclined to crash. When the nose is pointed downward, however, the plane follows suit and crashing is inevitable. The same is true in our lives. It's not the challenge we face that will determine how things will turn out; it is the attitude of our responses. It boils down to whether we will choose to be optimistic or pessimistic, victim or victorious. We can't allow impulsive, irrational, and illogical decisions to hinder our progress. This type of reaction will only push us further away from our destination. Responding to life with a can-do mentality changes everything. Remind yourself: "I *can do* all things through Christ who strengthens me" (Phil. 4:13 NKJV).

No matter what we go through in life, God chooses to see us as winners. He sees us overcoming our challenges and soaring to new heights. God never sees us as defeated or washed up. He wants us to have the same view. We can't get anywhere seeing ourselves as the victim of our circumstances. We have to believe that there is a brighter day ahead, even when we can't see it. There's always light at the end of the tunnel. The fullest sun comes after the worst storm.

God has blessed each of us with a beautiful gift—life. It is His desire that we enjoy it. To enjoy life to the fullest, we must choose to reflect on God's perspective of our lives. A lot of times problems continue to persist in our lives because we have the same negative thoughts about them. We see ourselves powerless rather than empowered. Even in our marriages and professions, we have to change the way we think to become successful.

CHOOSING A POSITIVE OUTLOOK

Many times, the hurdle in overcoming setbacks is regaining a positive attitude toward life after the storm. The things that have happened can't be relived. No matter how many times we rewind the tape, it can't be changed. So there is no point in looking back at it. Looking back causes us to get stuck in the past, and it hinders us from enjoying a better today. I've often heard my husband make the very powerful statement, "Stop rewinding the past and begin pre-playing your future!"

Rather than focusing on past or present circumstances, think about how you *want* life to be. Concentrate on the goals you want to achieve and the fact that you have been given a second chance at a better, more purposeful life. What happened yesterday may not have been fair; it may not have even been your fault. Some situations probably could have been avoided had the choices been different, but none of that can be changed now. We must learn from the past and embrace the future. When we fail to learn from the lesson, we are destined to repeat it. By learning from the experience, we position ourselves to grow, gain peace, and discover a positive outlook on life.

Acceptance is an important step toward staying positive. The "Serenity Prayer" says it best:

> *God grant me the serenity*
> *to accept the things I cannot change;*
> *courage to change the things I can;*
> *and wisdom to know the difference.*

To accept things in life doesn't mean that we *agree* or *consent* to the things that have happened. It simply means that we *acknowledge* it as part of our past. If I were to ask you if you were once a baby, I'm sure that you would say yes. The acknowledgement in no way indicates that you are still at that stage in life or that you act as a child now. It does, however, confirm that you were once at that stage, and without living through it, you could not have become the person you are today.

SURROUND YOURSELF WITH A
POSITIVE ATMOSPHERE

Earlier I reflected on the time when my mother went home to be with the Lord. That was an opportune time for me to become overwhelmed, bitter, and discouraged. The separation anxiety I experienced was tremendous! It all happened so quickly. Like the passing of the wind, she was gone. During that time, a well-meaning person said to me, "I was so excited when I heard about the passing of your mother." I'm sure he was trying to convey that my mother was in a better place and that she wouldn't have to suffer anymore, but it just rubbed me the wrong way. Sometimes we try to make people get to where we are too quickly. He was on the positive side of the big picture, but I was still in the middle of the moment. Healing is a process, and we have to be sensitive to that when we're trying to encourage people.

Of course, I was saddened by my mother's leaving, but that wasn't the time for me to be around people who felt sorry for me. I appreciated all the people who showed me compassion and love during that time. However, because I was hurting, I began to react. Just like the Israelites, I worried and complained. "Oh, God, why didn't You give her at least seventy years like You promised every believer?"

But the Lord answered me saying, "Thank Me that she lived as long as she did." It totally changed my perspective. I began to saturate myself in the Word every chance I got. I began meditating on the fact that mother had been a significant part of my past, and because she went to heaven, she would also be a tremendous part of my future.

Sometimes people become so buried in their grief that they never get beyond the experience. They hold on to it for years. Some turn their backs on God, the church, and the people who love them because they are angry or afraid to love again. I didn't want to be like that. I had to take control of my emotions to prevent them from ruining the rest of my life.

Many times, if we're not careful, we can prevent a breakthrough from occurring by having the wrong attitude. Granted, it's hard, and the situation may be unimaginable. We are emotional beings, and it is very difficult for us to press through those emotions. When things don't go as planned and people hurt or disappoint us, it's hard to see the light at the end of the tunnel. This is the time we must delve into the Word and stay close to God.

Hanging around positive people and listening to positive lyrics and messages can be a great help regardless of what is going on in our lives. Keeping a positive outlook should be a way of life. This is most easily achieved by keeping our environment filled with thanksgiving and praise. We must protect our eyes and ears by maintaining an environment that promotes our overall peace and well-being.

RULING OUT BITTERNESS

Here are a few tips I'd like to offer to help you avoid or overcome bitterness:

1. Replace your complaining friends with positive ones. Look at your circle of friends. Who's there? If you have friends who are always talking against their husbands or telling you what you should do, it's time to make a change. If you're hearing things like, "I'm so sick of my husband. He's no good. I called my attorney the other day. I'm just waiting on the papers to come in because he is lazy and sorry, and he's never going to change"; or if you have dreams that you want to accomplish and the friends around you say, "Give it up. You're too old for that now. You should have done that years ago," this is not the type of communication you should be exposing yourself to. You need friends who will build you up and support you. They should support your dreams and have a positive outlook about their own situations.

2. Replace fault-finding and complaining with thankfulness. Be thankful to God. I'm not suggesting that you thank Him for a bad situation or a difficult experience, but thank Him in the midst of it. God is your heavenly Father. There is no one like Him. He will work things out for you if you live a life of faith and trust Him. The fact that God is in your life means that you have far more working for you than against you. Thank Him daily and expect good things to happen. Your breakthrough is right around the corner.

The Bible says that we should do all things without complaining so that we will be blameless. (Phil. 2:14,15.) So change your words; they have power. Use that power for your good. Make a quality decision not to be emotionally ruled. Don't make decisions when you're emotional. Wait until after you've spent time in God's Word. Get His perspective, and allow His intervention in your situation.

3. Don't feed off of negative sources. We must learn to fix our minds on good things. Read positive books; listen to positive music, television, and radio. Surround yourself with people who are good for you and have your best interest at heart. If you've been bombarded with negative messages, make the change. Sometimes we just do things out of habit. We continue to listen to the news even though we don't have good feelings about it afterward. We stay for the next segment and the next. Don't get me wrong, we should be informed. But we can't allow the way we think to be determined by the messages the media portrays. Get the information you need, stay focused on what's good, and keep moving.

4. Commit to developing your spiritual walk. Attend church regularly. God wants us to surround ourselves with people who have similar thoughts and values to our own. He also encourages us to assemble with Christians regularly so that we may uplift each other. Prayer and meditation are also important. Get in a quiet place daily and talk with God. Listen as He speaks to your heart throughout the day. Seek Him for the answers you need, and meditate on positive thoughts.

5. Watch what you say. Words have power. So choose them carefully. If you want positive results, you've got to have positive communication. If you want negative results, complain and continue to talk about the things you don't want in your life. Either way, it's a choice. I encourage you to choose that which is positive.

Avoid quarreling, fighting, and gossiping. This type of communication produces strife and hinders every blessing. Instead, say good things. Learn to agree or agree to disagree; and don't take part in negative talk about anyone. Choose the high road. You'll be glad you did.

Dwelling on mistakes and living in the past can only hold us back. In every trial and every test, we must remember that God has already provided a way for us make it through. And we don't have to do it alone. He is there in the storm with us. Remember how Jesus calmed the raging sea when the disciples were in the ship? They were paralyzed with fear. When they called to Him, He answered and delivered them from trouble. The storm ceased in their lives when He said, "Peace, be still" (Mark 4:39 KJV).

In our own lives, we must cry out to God. There is no shame in calling out to the Father. He wants us to. Moses cried out to God several times. He could have panicked at the Red Sea. He could have also complained, "Lord, I did everything you told me to do. I went to Pharaoh over and over again until he set the people free. Now after all of that, you're going to let us drown?" He could have become negative and reacted by throwing up his hands just as the Israelites did so often in the wilderness. Instead, Moses responded in faith. When he cried out to God from the depths of his soul, God answered; and His provision prevailed.

Maintaining a positive outlook empowers us to achieve great things! It also helps us to connect to the authentic mindset God has given us to rise above obstacles in life. I encourage you to take the high road in every test you encounter from this moment forward. Choose to think positively. Cry out to the Lord and involve Him every step of the way. Don't go out on your own, and don't react. Respond with a positive outlook.

As we go through life, it is important that we choose our area of focus. Choosing a positive approach keeps us connected to the authentic lifeline of hope God has placed in each of us. Even through the most tedious moments in life, we must activate our faith by believing His Word. Focusing on positive solutions during difficult times helps us maintain a positive outlook on life, even when circumstances seem hopeless. By exercising our faith, we position ourselves to experience God's miracles.

- *Staying positive in a negative world is not easy, but it can be done. In fact, it must be done if we want our faith to continually increase. To live a positive life, we must intentionally focus our attention on good things.*

What makes it difficult for you to focus on the positive rather than the negative? What are some specific things about God on which you can choose to focus your attention?

_____

_____

_____

_____

Sometimes certain circumstances in life can shock us. What can you do to remain positive during setbacks or unforeseen events in life?

_____

_____

_____

_____

- *Sometimes the biggest challenge in dealing with our problems is understanding what to do and how we should respond. To find the answers, we must seek God and His perspective on our situation.*

What is the difference between *responding* and *reacting* to the situations we face in life?

_____

_____

_____

_____

What does it mean to trust God?

_____

_____

_____

_____

_____

_____

In what ways can you adjust your mindset to trust God even more where the issues in your life are concerned?

_____

_____

_____

_____

_____

_____

• *When it comes to having the right attitude, it is important to be careful not to put more faith in what you see going on around you than what the Bible says about your situation. Faith is all about trusting in God's ability to help you.*

In the midst of chaotic situations going on in the world, how can you maintain faith in God and His provision?

_____

_____

_____

_____

_____

Why is fear so dangerous to your faith?

_____

_____

_____

How do you handle negative circumstances?

_____

_____

_____

_____

- *When we respond to life's obstacles with great faith and determination, we reflect the true and authentic nature of God. It is generally in the darkest times that light is seen.*

Reflect on some of the difficult times in your life. How did you make it through? What would you have done differently (as it relates to your attitude)?

_____

_____

_____

_____

Do your current environment and associations support a positive outlook on life? How can you make adjustments in these areas?

_____

_____

_____

_____

_____

_____

_____

Chapter 3

AUTHENTIC SELF-LOVE

We have each been uniquely designed for a specific purpose. This is evident due to the fact that we have different personalities, gifts, skills, talents, preferences, and experiences. God never intended for us to be a clone of someone else. Therefore, we should embrace, love, and accept the masterpiece He has created each of us to be.

As we grow from childhood into adulthood, we go through different experiences—some positive and some negative. Regardless of how or why we go through some of these experiences, they are all usable by God. These experiences help to shape and mold us into the people that we become. As we grow and develop as individuals, we gain a concept of who we are and what we were created to do and achieve. Gaining a concept of who we are and loving ourselves unconditionally empower us to live an authentic lifestyle.

EMBRACING WHO YOU ARE

We must appreciate ourselves. Although it may not be a reality for some, when we look in the mirror, we should see one of the best people we know. It is important that we know ourselves better than we know anyone else—flaws and all—and that we are able to see ourselves as unique and exquisite individuals empowered by God to succeed in every area of our lives. We were wonderfully made by a loving God who does all things well. He purposely made us for a time such as this. Though others may resemble you and play some of the same roles as you, there is only one you. Only you can do what you have been created to do.

Knowing and loving who we are gives us the ability to live freely. When we take the time to appreciate the gifts and abilities placed within us, we can appreciate the gifts and talents of others. Taking the time to discover and develop the things that we are good at and interested in helps to nurture and cultivate our abilities so that we are always striving to be the best we can be for ourselves as well as for others.

Sometimes we run into challenges as we try to embrace our self-image on our journey to self-realization. Dealing with insecurities as a young woman almost prevented me from discovering God's plan for my life. As a result of my insecurities, I had to learn how to overcome the need to gain the approval of others, and I had to begin to see myself as God sees me.

Creflo would always encourage me to be more active at our church. He would say, "Taffi, you can do anything. You're a strong woman of faith. Step out, and do what God has called you to do!"

I would say, "Who, me? No way! You do your thing, and I'll be just fine." I was convinced that he was trying to make a preacher out of me; and, at first, I was against it. However, God revealed to me that it is His plan for me to minister to others, and He began to show me that I was allowing fear of what others would think of me to stop me from discovering and accomplishing all that God has created me to do.

While we need to be able to relate to others and enjoy their company, we must learn to do so without being oppressed by their opinions. This oppression is known as *people bondage.* I am so thankful that God helped me out of that struggle. Although there are times when it tries to return, I remind myself that I am free. In order to be free, I had a part to play in the process by arriving at an appreciation and acceptance of who I am as an individual. Through this self-realization, I was able to make a quality decision. Either I was going to remain the insecure person I had been for years, or I was going to be secure in who I was. I chose the latter, and once I started on my new journey toward self-acceptance and self-love, I began to focus on fulfilling my God-given purpose.

This reminds me of the story of Queen Esther. As a young woman, she was taken to King Ahasuerus' palace. The king, whose royal throne was the capital of the Persian empire, was looking for a new queen to replace Queen Vashti for disrespecting him. The king had his personal assistants search the empire for young virgins from which he would select the next queen. Esther, an orphan under the care of her cousin Mordecai, was one of those taken to the palace as a result of the king's decree. Before leaving for the palace, Mordecai warned her to keep the fact that she was a Jew to herself. While in the palace, the women went through a time of preparation for the king. During this time, by simply being herself, Esther won the admiration of all those who saw her. The king was totally fascinated by her. Because he was so in love with her, he chose her to become the new queen. Later, Esther learned that the king had issued orders to have all of the Jews killed. Because God was with her, she had the courage to not only reveal her true identity (as a Jew) but also go to the king and ask that he spare her people. Because Esther was secure in who she was, she accepted the challenge ahead of her, confident that God was able to use her in His purpose. At the time, no one else was in a position to save her people. When she first came to the king's palace, she had no idea that God was going to use her in that particular way. We are only capable of seeing where we are today, but God is able to see the bigger picture. He already knows when, where, and how we will make our mark in the world as we yield to His plan of self-acceptance and self-love. Being true to ourselves and allowing God to use us where we are positions us to be true and authentic vessels, which He can use in even greater ways.

ELIMINATE THE INNER CRITIC

Our self-esteem or self-worth is primarily based upon how we feel about ourselves. Because it is based on our emotions, it is usually expressed or reflected in what we do and say. And many times, these actions help others form their opinions and thoughts about us. But we must be mindful that, while the thoughts and opinions of others do affect us, they do not make us who we are. We are who God says we are. Negative thoughts may enter our minds because of negative or hurtful words that may have been said to us by those we have loved and trusted. But we must combat those negative thoughts with positive ones.

Having a critical spirit or being overly critical means we have a negative outlook on life. With a grim outlook, our view of everyone and everything is accompanied with fault finding, harsh accusations, demeaning attitudes, and a tendency to unfairly judge ourselves as well as others. Critical people tend to look down on everyone in a negative way in an attempt to build themselves up. The word *critical* actually means to find fault or to judge with severity, often too readily.

Being critical is opposite to God's nature. He does not focus on the negative aspects of anyone or anything. He is love, and His very nature is to see the best in everyone and every situation. Therefore, we should not be quick to find fault but to believe the best. We do not have to be naïve and unrealistic. However, we can choose to see things from a positive perspective that agrees with God.

God does not condemn us; although, He does correct us. He is not looking for opportunities to punish us or make us feel bad about ourselves. He is not a God who is constantly analyzing and punishing us each time we do something wrong. Because He is a loving and merciful God, we, as His children, should be the same—loving and appreciating ourselves and others unconditionally. When we recognize we are being critical, we should take inventory of what we have been seeing, speaking, and hearing. If we have been around negative influences, we must make a decision to limit (or eliminate if necessary) those influences.

When we begin to read the Bible on a regular basis and understand God's character, our thoughts will agree with Him. We will begin to understand that if we are to walk with God, we must agree with His plan. God can, and will, use everything He has placed on the inside of us for His specific purpose.

Everything that makes us who we are—our gifts, talents, abilities, and experiences—is designed to benefit others. Our God is a relationship God. He created us to have a close and intimate relationship with Him. And out of that love relationship will flow true and genuine love for others as we pursue all that God teaches us and shows us through His written Word.

Staying positive is not always easy. I sometimes find myself complaining or thinking negatively about things that I feel didn't go as I thought they should have gone. But I quickly redirected my thoughts by choosing to think about something positive like God's goodness or a Scripture that puts me in a mood of thanksgiving and praise.

It is easy to stay positive when we consider all that we have. And we, as His children, were selected, out of all that He made, to be like Him. No matter what we may consider our weaknesses or flaws to be, we are still the apple of His eye, and we are His most prized creations.

In order to bolster self-love and conquer the self-doubt, here are some keys to loving yourself in a healthy way:

1. *Always Be Yourself.*

There is only one you. So be the best you, you can possibly be. You are an original. No one else can be who you are or do what you do.

2. *Take Care of Yourself.*

Be sure to take practical steps to take care of yourself. Eat healthy food, get plenty of rest, exercise, and pamper yourself. Set aside special time each week to treat yourself to something you enjoy, such as a movie, dinner, pedicure or manicure, or a nice drive in the country. Be good to yourself; you deserve it.

3. *Replace Negative Thoughts about Yourself with Positive Ones.*

Negative people would like nothing better than for us to believe the negativity that attempts to rob us of our self-esteem. We must realize that God is love and any doubtful thoughts that come to our minds are not from God. When negative thoughts come, we must immediately choose to stop those thoughts and choose to say good and positive things about ourselves.

4. *Do Things That Cultivate and Nurture Your Gifts, Talents, and Hobbies.*

Constantly work on sharpening your talents. Be a good student of learning and a faithful steward over your gift. You want to always be abreast of the latest information concerning your fields of interest so that you are always growing and improving.

5. *Speak Positive Affirmations.*

Speak positive and encouraging words over yourself each day. Set goals, and speak life to those goals by speaking faith-filled words that will bring those goals to pass. The Bible says the tongue can bring death or life. In others words, you will have what you say. Using Scriptures is a good place to start when beginning to create positive affirmations:

I am victorious!

I John 5:4 AMP

I can do all things through Christ who strengthens me.

Philippians 4:13 NKJV

I am more than a conqueror through Christ Jesus.

Romans 8:37

God loves me with an everlasting love.

Jeremiah 31:3

Nothing can separate me from the love of God.

Romans 8:35

My God shall supply all my need according to His riches in glory through Christ Jesus.

Philippians 4:19

6. *Surround Yourself with Positive People.*

Be sure to guard your eyes, ears, and mouth by surrounding yourself with people who will have a positive impact on your life. Be sure that you have people who are willing to share in and celebrate your successes.

7. *Pray.*

Never think anything is too small or insignificant to God. He is a friend that sticks closer that any brother. He wants to be our closest and dearest friend. We can talk to Him just as we talk to our friends and loved ones. And the best part is He's never unavailable. He is always waiting with open arms to hear about everything concerning us.

We have each been uniquely designed for a specific purpose. This is evident through our different personalities, gifts, skills, talents, preferences, and experiences. God never intended for any one of us to be a clone of someone else. Therefore, we should embrace, love, and accept the masterpiece He has created each of us to be.

- *Gaining the concept of who we are and loving ourselves unconditionally empower us to live authentic lifestyles. We must appreciate ourselves. It is important that we are able to see ourselves as unique and exquisite individuals, empowered by God to succeed in every area of our lives.*

What are some of the benefits of having a positive self-image, and how can it affect our relationships and interactions with other people?

_____

_____

_____

_____

_____

_____

What are the drawbacks of being in *people bondage*? How can you eliminate being overly concerned with what other people think about you?

_____

_____

_____

_____

Why is being critical so damaging to your relationship with God and others?

_____

_____

_____

_____

_____

- *Staying positive is a decision. Every day we are faced with situations that have the potential to affect our attitude negatively. However, we must choose the positive over the negative.*

What are some things you can do to boost your self-esteem?

_____

_____

_____

_____

What role does your thought life play in how you feel about yourself? What are your dominant thoughts about yourself?

_____

_____

_____

_____

_____

_____

What can you do on a regular basis to develop the gifts and talents God has given you?

_____

_____

_____

_____

_____

What does it mean to guard your heart, particularly where your relationships are concerned?

_____

_____

_____

_____

How do you deal with negative thoughts when they come to your mind? Evaluate what you could do differently to effectively deal with such thoughts.

_____

_____

_____

_____

_____

Chapter 4

MATTERS OF THE HEART

I want you to take a moment to let the statement I'm about to make resonate in your heart and mind: God wants to use you. That's right! The almighty God has a plan for your life. Sure, He can use this person and that person, but He also wants to use you. God created you for a specific purpose. You may already know His plan for your life and are actively living out your purpose.

But perhaps, in your heart, you have an unspoken desire to do more. God places His desires in our hearts. If you have been feeling restless or stagnant lately, it may be a sign that He is ready to take you higher in your purpose. If you are contemplating steps toward fulfilling the next level of God's plan for your life, but you are not sure how or where to begin, try going back to the last instructions He gave you. From my own experiences, I've learned that if you take the first step, He will guide you the rest of the way.

On the other hand, you may have a good idea of what God's plan is for your life, but you are struggling with accepting the assignment. Perhaps you are concerned that you are inadequate in some way or you don't have the right education, experience, or ability. Don't worry; He's created a masterful plan, and the training and help you need are all a part of His plan. Just walk in it. The Word of God says those He has called, He has also justified. So there is no need to try to convince God that you are not qualified for the job. And when you begin carrying out the work He has called you to do, there will be no reason to try to convince people that you are qualified. You are already justified. All you have to do is trust God, obey Him, and fulfill His will for your life.

Even if you have no idea what God wants to do in your life, it doesn't negate the fact that He has created a plan just for you. I don't know what your situation is today or what may lie ahead in the future, but I do know that He wants to do good works through you. The things you have said or done in the past are irrelevant. The Word tells us that whatever God started in the beginning, He wants to finish. Philippians 1:6 NIV says "He who began a good work in you will carry it on to completion." Now is the time to develop a genuine relationship with God, one where you are completely open about every aspect of your life.

TAKING OFF THE LIMITS

Developing an authentic relationship with God begins by talking to Him like a trusted friend. It is an honest and open exchange about who you really are, the way you feel about your life, and your genuine concerns. Even though He already knows everything there is to know about you, honesty is what He seeks. God is calling each of us to take an honest look in the mirror and be real about who we are and the relationship we have with Him. By choosing to be completely open, we remove the excess baggage we sometimes carry and discover the reality of our authentic selves.

When people let their guards down and begin operating in absolute honesty, they are typically surprised to find that they are not the people they have convinced themselves they are. If this happens to you, don't be alarmed. Self-examination is a great way to begin an authentic and rewarding relationship with the Father.

You may already have a great relationship with God and feel that you are completely honest with Him. That's wonderful! But have you been completely honest with yourself about yourself? Have you suppressed your true identity for so long that you have lost touch with the real person inside? Think about it for a moment. Is there another side of you that the world hasn't seen yet? Before the pressures of life set in, would you have taken risks that you shy away from now? Do you ever wish that you had the courage to do certain things, but your head convinces you to do otherwise? If you answered yes to any of these questions, it's time to begin peeling off the layers to the authentic you inside.

Sometimes we limit our conversations with God. We talk to Him about the things we want, the problems we need fixed, and the blessings and favor we want to accomplish the goals we are working toward. Many times we rely on previous experiences to resolve our issues. In other cases, we seek the advice of friends and family. As a result, there are only certain issues we reserve for God. However, the reality is that God created you. He knows everything there is to know about you—the things you say, do, and attempt to hide. However, none of these things matter to Him. God wants all of you!

Now is the time to take the limits off God and yourself. When you experience setbacks in life, put your confidence in the reality of God's Word rather than the problems you face. By exercising your faith in God and His Word and trusting Him to bring you through, you can begin to approach your circumstances with greater hope.

FACT AND TRUTH

Although it may not be intentional, I believe there are times when we turn our backs on God's Word. Sometimes we invest more time magnifying our problems than magnifying our God. We have a tendency to believe that we are the only ones going through something, and heaven and earth have to stand still until the problem is resolved. Far too often we breathe life into our problems by talking about them and focusing all our attention on them. Rather than looking to God's Word for the solution, we look to other people, past experiences, talk shows, and reality TV. Eventually, the problem becomes so big that it consumes us.

The Word of God is Truth. Other than God, the Bible is the only authentic source of hope and assurance. The Word has a solution to every problem. It is the final authority. The truth of God's Word has been tested and tried throughout the ages; It is infallible. There is a distinct difference between fact and truth. The fact may be that your health is in jeopardy, but the truth is God's Word says you are healed. Therefore, you should expect healing. The fact may be that your bills are behind, but the truth is God will supply all your needs. The fact may be that your spouse left, but the truth is God will never leave you nor forsake you. *Forsake* means "to abandon, desert, disown or give up on." God promises He will be with you through every season of life.

Instead of talking about the problem, talk about the solution. Speak God's Word concerning your situation. Yes, I mean literally *speak* the Scriptures. Psalm 103:20 says angels hearken to the voice of the Word. That means they can only carry out an assignment if you speak the instructions. So give them something to work with. Say it! The Bible also says life and death are in the power of the tongue. (Prov. 18:21.) Words have power. If you talk about things that are mostly negative, you will have mostly negative experiences. But if you concentrate on positive thoughts—things that are good, pleasant, and of a good report—you will reap the benefits of positive things happening in your life.

If you are dealing with a health issue, don't go around announcing it to everyone. Talk to God about it. Search the Bible for Scriptures concerning your situation, and begin speaking His Word daily. It is the ammunition you need for healing. Sharing the news with certain family members and close friends is fine, but it shouldn't be the biggest topic in your conversations with them. If they ask how you are doing, say something like, "Oh, I've had better days, but by the stripes of Jesus I am healed!"

To be clear, I'm not saying you should ignore or deny the facts in your life. No. If a problem exists, it must be properly and immediately addressed. I just prefer to believe the report of the Lord. Remember, how you respond to life's circumstances will determine your outcome. Some Christians misinterpret the verse that says, "Call those things that be not as though they were" (Rom. 4:17). So they stop wearing their glasses or taking their prescriptions. That may sound funny, but you wouldn't believe some of the stories I have heard. These are extreme measures. This is not how the Scripture should be interpreted. What it does mean, however, is that we should speak into existence the things we want and desire by giving more attention to that which brings positive results. Focusing on the negative doesn't do any good. When a problem exists, you want results. The Word of God brings results. By investing time in reading the truths found in God's Word and saying the Scriptures aloud, you encourage yourself and boost your confidence.

So many times we get caught up in our circumstances and begin thinking they are more real than the Word. Make no mistake about it; no problem is more real than God's Word.

Second Corinthians 4:18 tells us not to focus on the things we see, we should make a quality decision to focus on things we do not see; *The Amplified Bible* goes on to say that the things we see are temporary (brief and fleeting), but those that are invisible are everlasting. What does this Scripture mean, you may be wondering. Basically, it means that the circumstances of life are all subject to change, but faith is eternal. If you're broke, busted, and disgusted, or you're sick and need healing, don't focus on the fact of the matter. Instead, focus on the truth of God's Word that says, "Beloved, I wish above all things that thou mayest prosper and be in health, even as thy soul prospereth" (3 John 1:2 KJV).

Whenever things happen unexpectedly or there is a problem we cannot solve, we can bring God's Word into the situation. It has the power to change anything! It is important that we know the reality of God's Word to the point that it demonstrates the proof of His power in our lives. The Word gives us hope. With it, we can overcome the devastating effects of anger, depression, and even loss. God's Word has the ability to keep us from feeling trapped or stranded by the circumstances we face.

The Word of God also has the power to renew the mind. In other words, it has the power to influence the way we think or perceive our circumstances. Romans 12:2 NIV says, "Do not conform any longer to the pattern of this world, but be transformed by the renewing of your mind. Then you will be able to test and approve what God's will is—his good, pleasing and perfect will."

The world has its own way of doing things. It is a system, a certain mindset, pattern, or way of thinking, if you will, that totally opposes the Word of God. The Bible encourages us to avoid thinking the way the world thinks. As believers, we are overcomers. By faith we believe the best despite our circumstances. When we learn how to employ God's Word in our daily lives, we gain strength and direction.

Although we live in this world, the Bible reminds us that we are not of this world. In other words, we don't follow its practices. Our lives are based on the truths found in His Word. Satan is the god of this world. He is a liar, and his system—the world system—is built on deceit. It is Satan's full intention to draw people to him by causing them to doubt God and His Word. He has established a pattern of falsehood and phoniness. As a result, we have to be careful that we don't place more confidence in the world's opinions and beliefs than we do in God's Word. God is real, and His Word is real. He doesn't want us to get caught up in a form of thinking that opposes Him. One day, the world and everything associated with it will pass away, but the Word of God will stand forever!

BEING REAL

When we fail to turn to the Word, we subconsciously make a decision to turn away from it. The more we turn away from the Word, the more we turn our backs to the truth. As a result, we live in a perpetual state of deception and compromise. This causes us to be dishonest with ourselves, with others, and with God. As Christians, we can't allow compromise to rule over our lives. There is too much at stake.

One thing I've learned in my role as a minister is that you have to be honest with people. My husband and I minister to all types of people, not just church-goers. We reach out to drug dealers, politicians, prostitutes, celebrities, the homeless—you name it. But people don't want a whole lot of mumbo jumbo talk about Jesus if our walk doesn't reflect the talk. The world is hungry for someone who is real: someone who is honest and trustworthy.

The longer we continue doing things to impress people, the longer we delay our dreams and goals from materializing. When we get the response we desire from people, that is our reward. There is no need for God to get involved. As a result, we sabotage the reality of our Christian life and character. But there's something about doing things out of the integrity of our hearts that moves the hand of God over our situation. Pleasing Him should be the basis of our motives.

In order for God to use us effectively, our hearts must be pure toward Him. There has to be a high level of authenticity in our lives to demonstrate that we are who we say we are: God's sons and daughters. The God we serve is real! His Word is real. And when we learn to give it first place in our lives, the realness of who God is can be seen.

As believers, it is vital that we demonstrate genuine love in the way we conduct our lives. People don't care how many Scriptures we know or how often we attend church. They don't want to hear us quoting a whole bunch of Bible verses at them if we can't back them up with results. Whether we are on the job, at the beauty salon, or at a football game, they want to see how genuine our relationship with God really is.

Everything we do is fueled by motive. The motive can be positive or negative. However, negative motives cover up that which is authentic. The surest sign that we're operating with wrong motives is when we find ourselves doing things to influence how others perceive us. For example, we act a certain way around a person to keep them from running over us or overlooking our efforts. Or we may act a certain way toward another person because we want to demonstrate that we are as equally competent as they are. There are times when we choose to wear certain clothes for the sole purpose of influencing or impressing someone else. But God can't use us effectively when we are not true to ourselves. If we are constantly trying to manipulate people and take advantage of them, if we are doing things just to get noticed, we will never fully realize the magnitude and reward of God's great purpose in our lives. To reach our maximum destination and potential, we must learn to be real at all times.

Here are a few things you can look at in your own life to get a clearer picture of where you stand in your authentic Christian walk:

Look at the evidence in your life. What type of fruit are you bearing? Does it indicate that you are living an authentic life? Are you consistently reaping the benefits of God's favor and blessings, or do you have to manipulate things to obtain your goals?

Is the quality of God's Word operating in your life? Are you using God's Word to guide you through your situations? Is there a difference in how you handle the circumstances of life and how someone who is not a Christian handles theirs? In other words, are you using the tool God has given you? What is your relationship like with God when your lights are turned off and your food and money are low?

Second Corinthians 4:2 MSG admonishes us to refuse to wear masks and play games. We can get so used to wearing masks that we forget which one we're wearing sometimes. We go to church with our work face on or to work with our church face on. In the middle of a conversation with a friend, we accidentally put on the wrong game face, and everyone is confused. Learning to be genuine at home, work, and even church requires a major reality check.

God is concerned about our hearts because what's in our hearts is reflected outwardly. The Bible says only the pure in heart shall see God. (Matt. 5:8.) The mark of a pure heart is revealed when we do things in secret and not for public recognition. When we do something nice for someone without telling everyone about it, we demonstrate this attribute. These are the types of positive motives God rewards.

I like how the *Message Bible* addresses the issue of doing good deeds toward others. Here is what it says:

> Be especially careful when you are trying to be good so that you don't make a performance out of it. It might be good theater, but the God who made you won't be applauding. When you do something for someone else, don't call attention to yourself. You've seen them in action, I'm sure—'playactors' I call

them—treating prayer meeting and street corner alike as a stage, acting compassionate as long as someone is watching, playing to the crowds. They get applause, true, but that's all they get. When you help someone out, don't think about how it looks. Just do it—quietly and unobtrusively. That is the way your God, who conceived you in love, working behind the scenes, helps you out.

Matthew 6:1-3

I don't know about you, but I don't want the rewards of men. I want the rewards only God can give. I want to do things God's way and achieve the things He has called me to. Sure, I like impressing people, but I like impressing God most. If He is pleased with me, that's enough. God is always at work behind the scenes. You may not get the big fanfare with everybody taking note and acknowledging you for all the great things you've done and the sacrifices you've made, but heaven knows. And heaven is keeping record of all your good deeds. There is an account created in heaven just for us that reveals how we live our lives.

I want mine to reveal that I am doing everything I can to please the Father and fulfill His will for my life. I want to see the evidence of His blessing in my life now. It doesn't make any sense for me to be successful in certain areas of my life and inconsistent in the areas that matter most. I don't want to be a successful business woman and minister yet fail at being a good mother and wife. I want to see God in my home, in my business, and actively working in the lives of my children. Every part of me has to consistently line up with the reality of who I am to achieve God's best.

UNRESOLVED ISSUES

Many times, we don't get the results we want in life because of the things we carry in our hearts. The Word of God is true, and every one of Its promises is ours to possess, but we must settle the matters within our hearts so that we can live the authentic life He has called us to. Unresolved issues affect our hearts tremendously.

Sometimes we carry the burdens of past hurt, disappointment, offense, and unforgiveness in our hearts for years. The negative impact of bad experiences can be devastating. But holding on to the negative emotions we suffer or spending time trying to get back at someone for what they did to us only hinders our progress. As terrible and undeserving as the situation may have been, we have to find the strength to let it go.

I've seen people who refused to talk to each other because of something that happened ages ago. They are stuck in the past! Interestingly enough, the individuals can be very sweet and generous people, but the moment they see, think about, or even hear the name of the person who offended them, they lose it. Hatred wells up in their eyes, their hearts begin pounding, and they get mad all over again. Once they start talking about the incident that led to these defeating emotions, it may be hours before they are done. Can these people still be used by God? Of course. Can He use them effectively and consistently? No.

In situations like these, it is always best if someone takes the high road. God can use the person who finds the courage to shake off past offenses and move on. Sometimes the whole thing is just a misunderstanding. When and if the two people finally share their perspectives on what caused the wedge to form between them, they often learn that the way they remembered or perceived the situation was totally wrong. All that wasted time is gone and cannot be reclaimed.

In fact, some relationships are forever mended when one party decides that enough is enough. They make a quality decision to approach the other person, stop nursing the wound, and choose to forgive and forget. Whether the other person decides to accept the offer is totally up to them. But the person who takes the high road, in essence, releases the situation to God and is then able to move on with his or her life. At that very moment, God can move through that person in ways He was unable to do before when anger filled his or her heart.

Sometimes an apology is all that it takes. It doesn't matter whether the person who apologizes is really to blame. What matters to God is that the relationship is renewed between the two people who once held contempt for each other. Many times when we can't see eye to eye with a person, we just have to agree to disagree and let it go. When this happens, He can work through us.

Too often we waste precious years holding on to things that set us back. Sometimes we're mad about things that the other person did, and they have no earthly idea that there's even a problem. While we waste time rewinding the tape in our minds, they are going on with their lives and thinking nothing of it.

There are couples who have stood the test of time. Some who have decided that even after the heartbreak of infidelity, they want to stay together and work things out. These are people who realize the importance of the investment they have made in the relationship. And quite often, they are the ones who choose faith to move their mountains. Generally, the person who breaks the vow repents over and over again and promises never to commit adultery again. As hard as it is to muster up the courage to move forward, the other spouse chooses to remain in the relationship and offers his or her forgiveness.

Sometimes, however, attempts to repair a broken relationship are hindered by feelings of distrust, low self-esteem, or secret unforgiveness. They may say they forgive, but they really don't know how. As a result, in nearly every argument, they bring up their spouse's faults again and again. In addition to that, nearly every time a member of the opposite sex is present, the partner who experienced the hurt becomes suspicious. His or her mind begins to race as negative thoughts torture him or her. All of the old feelings begin to overtake them. Before they know it, they are in a state of withdrawal. Sadly, they respond to their spouse as if he or she has committed the wrong again, and eventually an argument follows. The person who thought he or she was forgiven is once again penalized for the mistake.

Our experiences in intimate relationships are the only things that we allow to hold us back. It can be a plethora of things. Maybe you were passed over for a promotion that you worked months to achieve only to see that position awarded to someone else. It could be a childhood experience that affected your relationship with your family. A parent, sibling, or other family member may have said or done something that discouraged you. Maybe someone failed to celebrate or support your hard work and achievements. Or it could be a deeper hurt that came as a result of verbal, physical, or sexual abuse. Perhaps you were neglected, abandoned, or rejected.

These things are difficult and sometimes require months or years of counseling before healing can occur. If any of these things have happened to you, or if you have experienced some other form of setback that you just can't seem to overcome on your own, seek reliable and experienced help. It's okay to ask for help. In fact, admitting that you have a problem or need help is the first step toward recovery. There are great counselors out there who can and will work with you through your difficulties. Healing is possible, and it is available to all, regardless of the situation. Don't allow your income or pride to prevent you from seeking help. There are several resources available through non-profit agencies, churches, and private and professional practices.

God really wants to use you. He wants to turn the ashes in your life into something beautiful. Will you let Him? Every day is an opportunity for you to release the things that have been holding you back. Even if you've only held on to negative feelings for a short time, too much precious time has been wasted rehearsing the past. Aren't you tired of it? Aren't you fed up with the burdens you carry? Release them to the Father. He wants to do more for you than you can possibly imagine.

What if someone took you to the top of a mountain one day and asked you to look below? There, right before your eyes, were all the things you ever dreamed of, every need and desire. Off in the distance you saw a man standing and facing you with His arms opened wide. You inquired who the stranger was, and he responded, "That's God, and these are all the things He's been holding for you. He is waiting for you, and He wants to do great things in your life."

What if this particular individual went on to say that God had arranged these things for you the moment you asked for them, but each time you decided to rewind the tape and hold on to past experiences, it prevented Him from releasing them to you? What if he shared how God's heart was heavy with sadness because He wanted to fulfill your desires, but you never answered the door when He attempted to deliver them? When you asked, "What do you mean?" he explained that on numerous occasions God had knocked on the door of your heart asking you to forgive the person who had offended you. He admitted that on occasion you considered God's request, but you had become so accustomed to allowing pain, offense, bitterness, hurt, and unforgiveness to define you, that rather than letting go of those feelings, you just stayed the same.

PLEASING GOD

To live an authentic life, our desires must be directed toward pleasing God. It will require adjustments that will affect the way we think, act, and believe. God knows who we are—the real person who exists under all the protective layers we have created. He knows the intent of our hearts and why we do the things we do. There is no need to pretend when we are in His presence. Those times when we do things in secret that we don't want anyone to know about, God already knows.

Change is a process. It doesn't just happen overnight. It is an ongoing metamorphosis that continues to unfold throughout our lifetime. Sometimes we just have to throw ourselves on the mercies of God and ask Him to intervene. Change begins with a decision. It's not something someone else can do for you; it must be initiated and carried out by you.

Consistency is the key to your breakthrough. When you begin working toward making the necessary changes in your life, start small. Don't bite off one huge chunk. Just do a little at a time, and celebrate each victory along the way. God really wants to use you. He has great plans in store for you.

If you have been pursuing goals that you know are not God-directed, it's time you make His will your priority. Everything you want and dream of can be found in His will. There are certain desires God has placed in you to do. Don't be afraid to do them. He has equipped you in every way, and He will not fail you. Sure, you will make mistakes along the way; God already knows that. When you fall, get back up again and keep going. There's an awesome future waiting for you.

You may say, "Pastor Taffi, it's a little late in the game for me. The dreams God gave me should have been started years ago. I got off track. Now it's too late."

Child of God, it's never too late. You may not have achieved the goals you had hoped to achieve yet, but God can meet you where you are. Oftentimes we fill our minds with thoughts of inadequacy and fear concerning right timing. Perhaps you planned to continue your education, purchase a new home, start a business, or pursue some other big dream; but for whatever reason, those hopes and plans have been delayed. After long periods of waiting, we sometimes feel that it is easier to just throw in the towel and give up on the things we hope for. But I'm here to encourage you today: don't give up. No matter what age you are now or the number of U-turns you've had to take to get where you are today, God still has a plan for you.

Go back to the last thing God told you to do. Repent to Him for not following through. He can still use you. Maybe the thing He told you back then isn't what He wants you to do now. He can place a new dream in you, a new desire to fulfill His will. Ask Him for His plan. He will reveal it to you. Don't get stuck on yesterday and the mistakes you made then. God is ever moving. Seek Him for the plan He has established at this season in your life. Trust me; He's not finished with you yet. God can and will use you if you give Him permission. All He needs is your cooperation to begin.

God created you for a specific purpose, and He has a wonderful plan for your life. You may already know His plan for your life and are actively living out your purpose. Or perhaps, in your heart, you have an unspoken desire to do more. By cultivating a genuine relationship with God, you position yourself to hear from Him and be led on the path He has already planned for you.

- *Developing an authentic relationship with God begins by talking to Him like a trusted friend. It involves being honest and open about who you really are, the way you feel about your life, and your genuine concerns.*

Even though God already knows everything there is to know about you, honesty is what He seeks. Is there any emotional "baggage" you are holding on to? Write down your response, and share it with the Lord.

_____

_____

_____

_____

_____

What do you feel are the benefits of letting your guard down with God?

_____

_____

_____

_____

What are some of the things you wish you had the courage to do but never have?

_____

_____

_____

How can you begin to foster open communication with God, even in the way you talk to Him?

_____

_____

_____

- **We must be careful not to invest more time in magnifying our problems than we do the solutions. The Bible provides the answers to every dilemma in life.**

How can you create a positive outcome when you are faced with a negative situation?

_____

_____

_____

_____

What can you do to boost your confidence in what the Bible says?

_____

_____

_____

_____

_____

What does it mean to renew your mind?

_____

_____

_____

_____

_____

- **In order for God to use us effectively, our hearts must be pure toward Him. Our lives must be authentic in order to demonstrate that we are who we say we are: God's sons and daughters.**

What should be the distinguishing characteristics of a Christian?

_____

_____

_____

_____

_____

_____

_____

_____

How can you know if you have the wrong motives for what you do?

_____

_____

_____

_____

What characteristics can help you determine if your walk with God is authentic?

_____

_____

_____

_____

_____

_____

_____

_____

_____

Why is God concerned about what is going on in our hearts? How
can you begin to get rid of unresolved heart issues?

_____

_____

_____

_____

_____

_____

What are some things you can do now to implement change in your life?

_____

_____

_____

_____

_____

_____

_____

_____

_____

_____

_____

Chapter 5

THE FRUIT OF THE SPIRIT: THE MARK OF AUTHENTICITY

What makes the believer truly authentic? What causes us to stand out in the midst of hatred and selfishness and love that has grown cold? The answer is simple—the love of God! The fruit of the Spirit, which is love, is like an orange that has many sections. This fruit of the Spirit is made up of different components, all of which form a unified whole. Galatians 5:22-23 KJV describes these different segments, "But the fruit of the Spirit is love, joy, peace, longsuffering, gentleness, goodness, faith, meekness, temperance: against such there is no law." When we develop in these areas, we become living, breathing representations of God's character. This is how others will know we have a genuine relationship with God. The fruit of the Spirit is a believer's distinguishing mark.

Bearing the fruit of the Spirit is one of the most important things to understand about developing a true and authentic relationship with God and others. As we spend time in the presence of God through studying His Word and communicating with Him through prayer, praise, and worship; developing and growing the fruit takes place. Our heart is a garden, and the Scriptures are seeds. Once we get those Scriptures in our hearts, they will take root and grow. As they do, we must continuously water and cultivate those seeds. We are then able to continue to produce beautiful fruit in our lives that others can admire and enjoy.

For instance, operating in meekness enables us to walk in humility. This is the opposite of pride. One definition of *pride* is "excessive self-esteem; conceit." Pride can also be looked at from the standpoint of having a mindset that considers our own way of doing things as the best and only way. Pride thinks it has everything all figured out.

When we entertain pride, we set ourselves up for failure because we allow no room for divine direction from God. I am sure we can all think of times when we thought we were doing right, but we turned out to be very wrong! When we talk about becoming authentic, it involves striving daily to conform to the image of God, and meekness is one of the things that helps us accomplish this.

Being meek is something that is often mistaken for weakness. When most people think of meek individuals, the image that tends to come to their minds are of people who are doormats or who never speak up for themselves. Neither of these descriptions gives an accurate picture of what meekness really is.

On the contrary, out of meekness comes patience and humility, which display true inner strength. This leads us to walk in temperance (self-control) so that we are not quick to fly off the handle when things don't go our way. It is having the ability to maintain the right attitude despite someone else's negativity. It does not mean knowingly allowing others to take advantage of us, but it does enable the love of God to go to work when we have been abused. To be meek is to be humble, mild, patient, and longsuffering.

Becoming genuine in our display of God's love toward others is not easy. It can be extremely difficult to maintain the right perspective and outlook when facing another person's negative words or actions against us or our challenging situations and circumstances. However, allowing our character to develop forms a foundation for success. It will also make us authentic representations of God to others.

Meekness is a particularly powerful force to put in motion when someone offends us. Anytime we choose to respond to negative situations with an aspect of God's love, we give Him room to come in and work out the situation for us.

This type of mindset is not overly concerned with making our perspective known, because we trust God to handle that for us. We do not try to push our ways, opinions, and ideas on other people, even though their thoughts and actions may be wrong. At the same time, being humble and meek does not mean feeling worthless or unimportant. True humility is simply concerned with taking God's course of action in every situation, which will always put others first.

When we are humble and meek, we recognize and understand we are nothing without God at the center of our lives. When we align our minds and wills with what the Bible says about us and how we should live, we are truly humble.

Jesus demonstrated humility throughout His life. His whole mission was to do the will of God. He humbled Himself by putting aside His personal feelings for the sake of a greater purpose—making the free gift of salvation available to every person on earth. He denied His personal feelings and emotions so that God's love could be put on display. He modeled a genuine relationship with the Father.

When we take on Jesus' mentality, the spiritual force of meekness is set in motion, rearranging situations around us for our good. Jesus said, in Matthew 11:29 KJV, "Take my yoke upon you, and learn of me; for I am meek and lowly in heart: and ye shall find rest unto your souls." What He is essentially saying here is that if we will choose to do things His way instead of our own, life will be a lot less stressful. God's way of doing things includes meekness and humility. If we can just untangle and detach ourselves from the things that hinder us—such as the wrong thoughts, mindsets, habits, and ways of doing things that cause us pain and stress—we will experience peace and joy like we have never known. And we will find ourselves handling the pressures of life more easily.

Jesus always demonstrated humility as He communicated with others. For example, He never allowed the negativity of his enemies to cause Him not to walk in love toward them. His responses to his critics and haters were clothed in truth yet tempered with love. He always acknowledged God as the guiding force in His life and the source of His strength and power. He lived a life that was totally dependent on God, every step of the way.

Even while enduring the pain and humiliation of the crucifixion, Jesus did not fall victim to pride, choosing to do things His way. We cannot even imagine the suffering He went through so we wouldn't have to pay the price for our sins. He experienced every negative emotion imaginable, yet He remained humble. He had the ability to destroy all His enemies that day, just by speaking one word. However, throughout the entire experience, He never said a word. He forgave those who were participating in His murder and followed through with the Father's plan. Because of His decision to stay in humility, He overcame sin and redeemed mankind.

THE TRAP OF PRIDE

Proverbs 18:12 says that pride comes before a fall, but humility precedes honor. Pride is so deceptive because it convinces us we can handle our lives better than God can. When we are prideful, we try to exist independent of God. Because we were all created in His image, it is not possible to live independent from our divine Source; however, this doesn't stop us from trying at times!

Pride can be subtle. It can creep in when we face situations in our lives that we feel we know best how to handle on our own, even though the way we want to handle it is not the best way. For example, when others hurt us, we may be tempted to deal with the issue by seeking revenge as a means of getting back at them. Or, in the area of finances, we may try to live beyond our means or portray an image we really cannot afford. Our pride will cause us to keep going into debt to support our lifestyles or to compromise our financial stability in order to create a certain image. Humility keeps us humble before God, which positions us to achieve maximum results in life.

Another attitude that is based on pride is the one that says, "I'm responsible for my success." It is when we think we have "arrived," so to speak. In and of ourselves, we can do nothing, but it is through the divine ability in us that we can accomplish all things. It is our acknowledgement of this truth that displays humility.

As a wife, mother, and pastor, I am constantly faced with situations where I have to make a decision about how I am going to respond. Sometimes it is more tempting to follow my emotions rather than choose love's way of doing things. But I always have to check myself and ask whether my response is going to be a prideful or humble one.

When we are faced with challenging emotional situations, we have to consider whether a particular word or reaction to a person or circumstance is going to demonstrate the character of God to others. Our lives are to be examples, and those around us are paying attention to how we respond to life's challenges. Usually, if our response is one that satisfies our own emotions or selfish desires, it is based on pride. Taking inventory of our attitudes and mindsets on a daily basis will help us locate ourselves and make the necessary adjustments.

LIVING A LIFE OF SELF-CONTROL

Walking in love is the opposite of selfishness, which is concerned with fulfilling our own desires. When we talk about developing the fruit of the Spirit, another component of it that directly ties into meekness is temperance. This is an area that requires development because it does not come naturally! In life, we encounter many different types of people and situations that require us to exercise self-control, which is why temperance is so important.

Temperance is defined as "moderation in one's appetites or emotions; restraint." Having restraint is critical because it demonstrates that our feelings do not determine how we respond to life. The temperate person is the one who has control over his reactions.

God doesn't want us to be out of control when it comes to our actions, but how we act begins with the way we think. Our thought life is the starting point for everything we do; it is like a control center. If we constantly think about doing and saying things that do not please God, we will eventually act on those thoughts.

The opposite of temperance is lasciviousness, which is having a lack of restraint, or not being able to find the brakes when it comes to a certain behavior. When you feel you are no longer in the driver's seat of your life, it is time to let temperance go to work.

There are many areas in our lives where restraint may be necessary. From the words we speak to our eating habits, self-control keeps us from losing control. But again, habits begin as thoughts left unchecked. When we have thoughts that do not line up with what the Bible says, we cannot choose to allow them to run wild in our minds. Instead, we must reject them by speaking a Scripture that deals with that particular thought or situation.

Temperance ultimately boils down to making the Bible your final authority in life, which pleases God and translates into a real relationship with Him. First you have to find out what the Bible says about the things you're dealing with, and make a note of them. Do you need self-control where your eating is concerned? If so, find out what the Bible has to say about your situation. Do you find yourself frequently losing your temper? The same concept applies. Once you have a list of Scriptures, begin to spend time each day thinking about them. Consider how you can apply the words to your life and the situations you are going through. If you lack self-control in a particular area, use the Scripture as your standard.

Practicing temperance is not always easy. But through renewing your mind, you can change the way you think about it. Romans 12:1-2 says that we are transformed through the renewing of our minds. Cussing someone out may satisfy our emotions, but it doesn't reflect God's love. Keeping our mouths shut and praying for the person who offended us may be more challenging, but it shows godly character.

Developing temperance requires a two-pronged strategy. First, we must learn to control our mouths, and second, we have to strengthen our inner man or our spirits. Putting restraints on our words is challenging because so many of the words we speak and our patterns of conversation have become habit. So monitoring our speech takes discipline and awareness at all times. When we find ourselves saying something we know does not line up with the Bible, we should check ourselves immediately. Becoming conscious of what is coming out of our mouths is crucial.

Spending time reading the Bible also cultivates temperance. Just like our physical bodies need food for nourishment and strength, our spirits also need "food." The Bible provides us with the spiritual fortitude we need to overcome temptation and get rid of our old ways of thinking.

Finally, we have to be determined to walk in temperance. And the greatest motivation to do this is the fact that it pleases God. When we are determined to walk in the love of God and develop the fruit of the Spirit, it pushes us when we don't feel like doing the right thing. It is the attitude that refuses to quit or give up in the process of change.

It takes discipline to exercise self-control, so find an area of your life in which you need more restraint and commit to temperance. Once you master one area, you'll discover it is much easier to take on another. Pretty soon, you will find yourself living a lifestyle of self-control. This is not to say you won't have moments when you slip and miss the mark—we all do. But when you do, simply ask God to forgive you and keep moving forward.

I don't know about you, but I want everything God has to offer. I want to experience the very best in life, and I want to let others know that they, too, can take part in all the good things that come with living for God. Making the effort to change the way we think is a small price to pay for the total-life prosperity that is available to those who dare to do things God's way. When we purpose to walk in the fruit of the Spirit, we are taking the road of humility, which has a blessing attached to it. And when our behavior is influenced by the love of God at all times, we become true representations of what it means to be true Christians.

What makes the Believer truly authentic? The answer is simple— the love of God! The fruit of the Spirit is love, and it has different components—joy, peace, longsuffering, gentleness, goodness, faith, meekness, and temperance. When we develop in these areas, we become living, breathing representations of God's character. The fruit of the Spirit is a Christian's distinguishing mark.

- *Bearing the fruit of the Spirit is one of the most important things to understand about developing a true and authentic relationship with God and others. As we spend time with God, we will begin to develop the fruit in our lives.*

What are some ways you can spend time with God that will help to develop the fruit of the Spirit?

_____

_____

_____

_____

Why does bearing the fruit of the Spirit make a believer authentic?

_____

_____

_____

_____

_____

_____

What is the difference between pride and humility? How can you tell if you are operating in either one?

_____

_____

_____

_____

_____

How can you maintain the right attitude in the face of others' negativity?

_____

_____

_____

_____

_____

What are some examples of how Jesus maintained an attitude of meekness and humility?

_____

_____

_____

_____

- **When faced with challenging emotional situations, it is easy to allow our feelings to take the driver's seat in our lives. However, we must remain focused on God's Word, using It as the standard for how we respond.**

Think of a situation in which you reacted emotionally. Which aspect of the fruit of the Spirit was needed in that situation?

_____

_____

_____

_____

_____

What is an area in your life where you need to develop temperance?

_____

_____

_____

_____

_____

What role does your thought life play in maintaining self-control?

_____

_____

_____

_____

_____

_____

What two areas are most critical when it comes to developing temperance?

_____

_____

_____

_____

_____

What does it mean to renew your mind?

_____

_____

_____

_____

_____

Chapter 6

ESTABLISHING AN AUTHENTIC RELATIONSHIP WITH GOD

Have you ever heard the phrase, "Come as you are"? Usually it is in reference to being invited as a guest to an event or function. It implies being able to attend without any regard to any exterior factors such as clothes or other outward appearance. It communicates that you will be accepted as you are, no questions asked, and that your authenticity is welcome. Did you know God looks at us the same way? He desires a genuine relationship with us, one in which we come to Him on a regular basis, just as we are. Our ability to fellowship with God without reservation and pretense is what gives genuineness and trust to our interaction with Him.

When something is genuine, it is real and sincere. This is the type of relationship everyone aspires to have with their loved ones. Think about the level of security you experience with a person with whom you know there are no ulterior motives. You can let your guard down, be yourself, and allow them access to the more intimate parts of your life without fear that they will somehow take advantage of you. Authenticity is critical to successful relationships.

I believe establishing a genuine relationship with God begins with looking at what is going on inside of us—in our hearts. The *heart* refers to the core of who we are. To gain concept of it, we can draw a parallel to the natural, human heart. From a physical standpoint, the heart is responsible for keeping us alive. Without it functioning properly, our bodies would shut down. Well, the same is true with our spiritual "heart." It is the place from which the issues of our lives originate (Prov. 4:23).

When our inner man is strong and free of negative emotions that can pollute our spirits, we are able to have a more intimate relationship with God because there aren't a lot of things getting in the way of our interaction with Him. Many times the things we carry deep within are what hinder us from having healthy, productive relationships with others. Pain, rejection, and fear can cause us to put up walls that lock others out of our lives. The same is true where our relationship with God is concerned. The hidden issues of the heart can keep us from enjoying Him to the fullest extent.

God is the author of relationships, and how we relate to our Creator really shows how we will relate to those around us. Having a genuine relationship with God means getting honest with ourselves about where we are and what we are dealing with inside. He knows us anyway, so instead of trying to hide or smooth over those deep heart issues that need healing and correction, we should be real with ourselves and God about them.

When I talk about heart issues, I'm talking about those things that create a rift in a relationship. If you think about it, things like strife, unforgiveness, and selfishness can ruin our relationships with people. They can also affect our relationship with God. These negative emotions can influence our behavior and get us in a position outside the love of God. When this happens, we tend to shy away from Him because we know we are carrying negative emotions. And since God is love, we go against the way He created us when we harbor these types of emotions.

Becoming genuine means acknowledging rather than ignoring what is going on inside of us. If we are ever going to get to a place of liberty and peace with ourselves and God, we have to bring everything we are carrying to Him. We can even ask Him to reveal our heart condition to us so we can know and understand what it is we have been holding on to. Many times we are unaware of how deep the issues are. However, when we become aware of them, we can then ask forgiveness and release our shortcomings to God. He is faithful to restore our souls and give us a pure heart. It is in the presence of God that we experience the freedom that comes from being honest with Him about what is going on in our lives.

The most important thing we can do to maintain a genuine relationship with God is to guard our hearts. We can do this by:

1. *Praying daily.*

Talking to God is a great way to foster a good relationship with Him. Anytime is a good time to talk with Him. He is always there, ready and willing to listen. I talk to the Lord like I would to a good friend! I also declare what He has said in His Word about whatever

I may be going through or have to deal with. Even when I'm not going through some type of negative situation, I gain a lot of insight through prayer.

2. *Refusing to dwell on our mistakes.*

Harboring guilt and condemnation disrupts our fellowship with God. None of us are perfect. When our lives are off track or we have missed the mark in some area, we have to keep moving forward. Blaming ourselves and holding on to past mistakes only slows down our progress.

3. *Blocking every negative channel.*

It is really important to avoid environments and people who are consistently negative. Those who can't see beyond their mistakes won't be able to help us see beyond ours. What and who we surround ourselves with have the potential to affect the way we think—positively or negatively. When we choose to concentrate on the good, we can expect good things to happen.

4. *Allowing God's Word to guide us.*

The Bible contains answers to life's most difficult questions; It is the roadmap to our success. We must take time daily to read and consider Its truths. Over time, it will affect our hearts and minds in powerfully positive ways.

Sometimes we have a view of God that comes from harsh religious beliefs and traditions. These types of mindsets actually prevent us from feeling free to come to Him without fear. We tend to think of Him as a mean God who is waiting to strike us with a lightning bolt when we do something wrong. However, the truth is, God is love; it is who He is! We can know Him as the loving Father that He is, picture Him welcoming us into His open arms and giving us a big hug. We can also imagine Him reaching into our hearts and pulling out the things that hurt. When we come to God in this way, He is always waiting for us to take the first step.

PASSION: THE HEARTBEAT OF RELATIONSHIPS

Any good relationship takes energy from both parties involved. If only one is putting forth the time and effort needed to maintain the communication, there is imbalance. Many times we look at God as a distant, impersonal Being without realizing He is a real person who has feelings just like we do. His desire is to personally interact with us on a continuous basis. He wants to guide and direct our lives, take care of all our needs, and, most of all, lavish us with His love.

I don't know about you, but when I think about the goodness of God, I get excited; and it makes me want to give my all to Him. When I get up each morning, I thank Him for allowing me to see another beautiful day, for a sound mind, good health, and a wonderful family. I think about all the awesome things He's done for me in life, and it makes me want to love Him even more. His mercy and unfailing love for us are reasons to be passionate about our relationship with Him.

When I think of passion, what comes to my mind is the idea of having intense emotions. From relationships to personal dreams and goals, passion is the fire that keeps things going. Think about it, a passionless life is dull and boring. And if we do not have passion for what we do, there is no motivation to keep doing it! The same is true in our relationship with God. Authentic spirituality is marked by strong enthusiasm. With each new day comes brand new opportunities to develop passion for God and to allow that passion to take our relationship with Him to higher levels.

Our emotions are what determine our passion for someone or something. How we feel about a particular thing makes us want to go "all the way" for it. For me, my feelings for God and the desire to live a life that demonstrates love toward others are what drive me to do what I do in life. It is the fuel that gives power to my relationship with Him.

I often teach on the importance of dealing with our emotions in a healthy way and recognizing that they are not all bad. Emotions in and of themselves are not destructive, but it is what we do with those emotions that makes the difference. For example, negative emotions, if acted upon, can drive us to make bad decisions. On the flip side, emotions can also enable us to express feelings of love and care toward people. In addition, they also allow us to "feel" after God. This simply means we can allow our emotions to draw us close to God and fully experience Him in a deep and meaningful way.

Feeling after God is essentially what helps us increase the passion level of our relationship with Him. As I feel after God, I allow my emotions to propel me toward Him. Love, adoration, peace, and joy are all produced and developed while in His presence. When I feel after Him, He becomes the main focus of my emotional energy, which deepens my desire to be closer to Him as I seek to know more about Him and to please Him.

Spending time in the presence of God is essential to developing an authentic relationship. It also builds trust and security. Consider for a moment your closest, most trusted friends. When you reflect on how you got to that level of closeness, you realize it came as a result of spending a lot of time with them, getting to know their character, and building trust. You let your guard down and allowed them into your world, and they did the same with you. When you are in a relationship with someone, time spent together is of the utmost importance. An intimate connection cannot exist without it.

The same is true where God is concerned. We were all created to have intimacy and closeness with God that exceeds any relationship we have ever known. When He is the primary focus of our passion, our love for Him is reflected in all our other relationships as well. The love of God will fill and flood our hearts, spilling out into our interactions with others on a daily basis. People will see our light and feel our love for them. This light and love come only as a result of spending time with God each day.

I like to make my personal time with God a priority because it really helps shape the course of my day. Devotional and prayer time are great ways to quiet our inner-selves and allow God to strengthen our spirits. Spending time in the Word is also important because it allows us to discover God's character and plan for our lives. The more we get to know Him and see how good He is, the more passionate we become about having Him in our lives.

LIGHTING THE FIRE OF LOVE

One of the things I am becoming more and more passionate about in life is sharing the love of God with others. And again, this desire is born out of love for God and wanting people to know how much He loves them. There are a lot of hurting people out there who have been bruised and wounded by their life experiences. We live in a cruel world that does not provide comfort from the storms of life. People are looking for answers, and each of us is a puzzle piece in the big picture. By lighting the fire of love within us, we can each make an impact in the lives of people everywhere.

When God spoke to me about starting the Prestige ministry, an outreach that focuses on reaching women who work in the sex industry, I wondered how I would carry out the vision He had given me. I didn't have the complete plan mapped out, but I did have a burning desire to be a blessing to women who wanted other alternatives to this lifestyle. God began to bring women to me who had the same passion and love for people that I did to be a part of the Prestige team. And He continued to lead us as we started this new ministry.

As Prestige began to take shape and our visits to the clubs and streets of Atlanta became regular occurrences, my love and compassion for people began to grow even more. Loving others is my all-consuming passion. It has become the reason why I do what I do.

I believe we all should allow that love for people to permeate every aspect of our lives, from our speech to our actions. We have the ability to love anyone, despite what they may do or not do. It starts with our love for God, and that love for Him then flows into our interactions with others.

There are some really powerful passages in the book of 1 John that talk about how loving others is what makes our relationship with God genuine. First John 4:7 KJV says, "Beloved, let us love one another: for love is of God; and everyone that loveth is born of God, and knoweth God." And verses 20-21 say:

> If a man say, I love God, and hateth his brother, he is a liar: for he that loveth not his brother whom he hath seen, how can he love God whom he hath not see? And this commandment have we from him, That he who loveth God love his brother also.

Being a person whose heart is burning with God's love for others is what draws people to you. And sincere love can be readily perceived and felt. The same is true where phoniness is concerned. As Christians, we are catalysts of change, and it is our authentic relationship with God, evidenced by our love for others, that will bring about transformation in the lives of others.

Matthew 5:16 says that those who belong to God are to allow their light to shine so everyone can see it. Wanting others to know about God and showing them who He is, are also signs of a passionate heart. We should strongly desire people to come to a knowledge of God and the blessed life that is available to them through a relationship with Him.

Demonstrating our passion for God is not difficult; in fact, we probably have opportunities throughout our day to do so. When we slow down a little, we are able to identify divinely arranged opportunities that God gives us to allow our light to shine on those around us. Too often we brush people off, rushing here and there and missing those precious chances we have to be a blessing to someone through our words or actions. But those are the moments that make our true character evident.

Honesty, not perfection, is what God desires from us. He simply wants us to be real about who we are and to express love toward others. It is the condition of the heart that determines the type of relationship we have with God. He desires that we have open communication and fellowship with Him. Being true to Him and ourselves empowers us to be true with others. He is a loving God who constantly showers us with His blessings and favor. He wants us to win in life, and when we cultivate an authentic relationship with God, we cannot fail.

Have you ever heard the phrase, "Come as you are"? It communicates that you will be accepted as you are, no questions asked, and that your authenticity is welcome. God desires a

genuine relationship with us, one in which we come to Him on a regular basis, just as we are. Our ability to fellowship with God without reservation and pretense is what gives genuineness and trust to our interaction with Him.

- *Establishing a genuine relationship with God begins with looking at what is going on inside of you in your heart. Negative emotions toward God, yourself, and others act as roadblocks which hinder your ability to have true fellowship with the Lord.*

Can you identify any negative emotions you may be holding in your heart toward God, yourself, or others? How did they originate?

_____

_____

_____

_____

_____

_____

How can the hidden issues of the heart keep you from enjoying your relationship with God to the fullest extent?

_____

_____

_____

_____

- **There are specific things you can do to foster a genuine relationship with God. Prayer, spending time in the Word of God, eliminating negative relationships and environments, and refusing to dwell on past mistakes are key components of true and intimate fellowship.**

What can you do to enhance your prayer time with the Lord?

_____

_____

_____

_____

Why are guilt and condemnation so detrimental to your fellowship with God? What can you do to eliminate these negative emotions in your life?

_____

_____

_____

_____

Evaluate the people with whom you surround yourself. Locate any negative influences in your life. How can you begin to eliminate these influences in order to have a more fruitful experience with God?

_____

_____

_____

_____

_____

What types of mindsets can prevent you from having a productive relationship with God?

_____

_____

_____

_____

•   **Healthy relationships are a two-way street. It takes the consistent effort of both parties to make things work. What you put into your relationship with God determines what you get out of it. He is waiting to engage in a flourishing relationship with you.**

In what ways can you develop and maintain passion for God and other people?

_____

_____

_____

_____

Chapter 7

THE TRUTH ABOUT LOYALTY

What does loyalty have to do with being an authentic Christian? What does it have to do with succeeding in life as a Christian? First, let's define *loyalty*. Loyalty is faithfulness and dependability. Another definition says that it is affection or high regard. We cannot simply say that we are loyal. Loyalty is demonstrated by our actions.

Generally, we see what can be perceived as loyalty all around us. Football fans are loyal to their favorite football teams. We see them often wearing their jerseys and getting into intense discussions about past and future games. They are usually the ones screaming enthusiastically throughout the games, and they wouldn't dream of missing a single one. Many students wear their high school or college apparel or purchase other school memorabilia. And still others sport the emblems of their sororities or fraternities. These are just a few examples of how we tend to express our loyalty and affection for things we are interested in and attached to in some way.

Loyalty and faithfulness are important and essential to an authentic lifestyle. When we become Christians, God helps us to be faithful. I often tell my story of how God helped me to be faithful as a single Christian woman. When I was in college, I began my personal relationship with Jesus Christ. I then began seeking His plan for my life. As I learned more about the Bible, I became committed to remaining pure and dating in a way that was pleasing in God's eyes. When I met Creflo, both of us had made the commitment to live according to the standards God set in the Bible. We knew He didn't want us to fornicate or get into any type of sexual immorality. He was faithful in helping us abstain from sex during the three years we dated before we got married. Through our loyalty and commitment to God and each other, we were able to develop and sustain the friendship we still enjoy today.

As we commit and purpose in our hearts to be faithful and loyal people, we can be sure that we will reap the benefits of our choices and decisions. Even if we may not see the results right away, if we are patient and determined to endure, we do reap what we sow.

FAITHFULNESS IN RELATIONSHIPS

If our relationships are to be true and authentic, loyalty must be present. Our relationships are very important in our lives. God is a relationship God. He created us to have a relationship with Him. Each of us is important to Him, and He desires to know each of us intimately. Along with our relationship with Him, He has also blessed us to have relationships here on earth to enrich our lives and bring joy to them. There are all types of relationships that can be formed in our lives. Many of them are the close and personal ones we share with family and friends. Then others are professional, formal, and informal, depending upon the situations and the circumstances. Our level of commitment to these relationships is, of course, based upon how intimately we know the individuals and how much weight the relationship carries in our lives. Those relationships that we hold dear to our hearts are usually formed very early in life and often last for many years. Over time, mutual trust and respect are established upon which love and commitment are built. As a wife, mother, daughter, sister, aunt, pastor, and friend, I have established relationships that I hold very close to my heart. And while each of these people that I am connected to knows that I love them and care for them, it is not enough to show this love through just my words only. As a person who is committed to these relationships, it is my responsibility to show them through my actions that I am faithful and committed to them and to our relationship. As Creflo would say, I desire to give them the advantage instead of taking the advantage. Our relationships take work. But if we are committed to honor those we love with our time and effort, the rewards are truly worthwhile.

Confucius once said, "To all you serve, be loyal." This is indeed timeless wisdom that is certainly still relevant even today. As Christians, we are servants. Oftentimes, we find it easy to serve those with whom we have personal relationships, but we have also been commissioned by God to serve others as well. Aside from our personal relationships, we still have professional and formal relationships with people we see on a regular basis that we are connected to for different reasons. These relationships include acquaintances, coworkers, supervisors, neighbors, fellow church members, etc. Although these are not people that we know intimately, as His servants, it is the will of God that we serve others. Although it may be difficult to remain loyal to those who are difficult to love, we can always pray for assistance as we strive to be loyal and committed in these relationships.

As I've said before, we are God's representatives on the earth. And as such, we are living reflections of our Father. When others see us committed and faithful to our spouses, children, bosses, coworkers, family, and friends, we set a standard of excellence that others will often admire and reciprocate. Because we are dedicated and committed—true to our word and trusted to always come through—it will compel others to be the same for us. And while this should not be our main objective for being faithful and loyal in our relationships, it will surely be a benefit that we can truly enjoy.

I believe that the same amount of effort we put into something is exactly what we can expect to get out of it. In other words, our actions determine our satisfaction in our endeavors. Trusted and dedicated service yields favorable and pleasing results.

Faithfulness is actually something God equips us with when we accept Jesus Christ as our Savior. He places within us the ability to be faithful as well as other characteristics modeled after His own character. Those characteristics are the fruit of the Spirit. As believers, we have on the inside of us divine love, joy, and peace, as well as all the other spiritual gifts that empower us to live authentic and abundant lives.

FAITHFULNESS IN RELATIONSHIP WITH GOD

The loyalty, commitment, reliability, and faithfulness we display in our relationships reflect the type of relationship we have with God. Spending time with God is vital to an authentic lifestyle. However, sometimes the busyness of our day-to-day routine takes over, and time with God seems difficult to chisel in. However, God is always interested in what is going on in our hearts. If we love and respect Him, we will willingly and joyfully serve Him. When we faithfully serve God, we will reap good results in our lives.

There are so many benefits to spending time with God. The more loyal or dedicated we are to spending time with Him through reading the Word and prayer, the more we become like Him. His character becomes our character. Making Him our closest confidant keeps us in good company.

I'm sure you have heard the saying, "We are known by the company we keep." This statement is so true. Those friends that we spend the most time with are the ones who most likely influence us the most, and they are also the ones others identify us with. This is why it is so important that we stay in the presence of God. We want others to easily identify us with the divine company we keep. As we spend more time with Him, His faithfulness to us becomes more real in our lives. And as a result, that faithfulness is reflected in us and displayed to others.

Finding time to spend with God should not be stressful. Being faithful to the relationship simply means that we are in constant and consistent communication with Him. Whether on the go or in the comfort of our own homes, spending time with Him simply means we acknowledge Him and communicate with Him throughout each day. As we fellowship with Him this way, we begin to get to know Him better. He will begin to share with us the things that are on His heart, which will enable us to live our lives according to His plan.

Throughout the Scriptures in the Bible, we see a constant theme: faithful and diligent people get His attention. He is willing to show up and shower the diligent with favor, power, and His goodness! The Scriptures are clear in their messages concerning how we are to live:

- "A faithful man shall abound with blessings, but he who makes haste to be rich [at any cost] shall not go unpunished."
Proverbs 28:20 AMP

- "The hand of the diligent shall bear rule: but the slothful shall be under tribute." Proverbs 12:24 KJV

- "He becometh poor that dealeth with a slack hand: but the hand of the diligent maketh rich." Proverbs 10:4 KJV

- "Most men will proclaim every one his own goodness: but a faithful man who can find?" Proverbs 20:6 KJV

- "He who diligently seeks good seeks [God's] favor, but he who searches after evil, it shall come upon him."
Proverbs 11:27 AMP

- "His lord said unto him, Well done, good and faithful servant; thou hast been faithful over a few things, I will make thee ruler over many things: enter thou into the joy of thy lord."

  Matthew 25:23 KJV

- "Now, a person who is put in charge as a manager must be faithful."

  I Corinthians 4:2 NLT

Faithfulness, loyalty, and commitment are essential to any life, regardless of who we are or where we are in our lives. Our decision to be faithful and committed individuals sets a standard in our lives that places us in a position to bless others as we, in turn, are blessed ourselves. God expects us to be loyal and committed in all that we do, and if we need His help, He is faithful to help us if we ask Him to.

We are God's representatives in the earth. As such, we are living reflections of our Father. When others see us committed and faithful to our spouses, children, family, friends, bosses, and coworkers, we set a standard of excellence that they will often admire and reciprocate. Loyalty is essential to our lives as Christians. God is faithful, and we are made in His image. Therefore, if we are to imitate Him in how we live our lives, we must be sure we are found loyal in all we do.

- *Loyalty is faithfulness and dependability. Loyalty can also be defined as affection and high regard. Loyalty cannot be demonstrated by our words; it is seen through our actions. In other words, we cannot simply tell someone we are loyal. We have to prove it to them over a period of time.*

In what ways do you show loyalty to your favorite things or activities, such as your favorite football team, TV show, college, club, etc.?

_____

_____

_____

_____

_____

_____

_____

_____

What other things stir your passion?

_____

_____

_____

_____

In what other ways do you express your loyalty and affection to the things you are passionate about?

_____

_____

_____

_____

_____

_____

• *When we become born-again Christians, God helps us to be faithful in our relationship with Him and others.*

As a Christian, in what ways has God specifically helped you to be faithful to His Word?

_____

_____

_____

_____

How has God helped you to be faithful and dependable in your relationships?

_____

_____

_____

_____

_____

_____

Have you had people in your life who have not been faithful and dependable? Who are they?

_____

_____

_____

_____

Have you forgiven them?

_____

_____

What have you learned from their mistakes?

_____

_____

_____

_____

• *Most of us have close relationships with family and friends who enrich our lives in some way, and over the years, we have had opportunities to grow in trust, respect, and love for them.*

List the people in your life whom you hold dear to your heart.

_____

_____

_____

_____

_____

Would your loved ones call you faithful and dependable? Why or why not?

_____

_____

_____

_____

Are there ways in which you can be more loyal in those relationships?

_____

_____

_____

_____

_____

_____

Are you willing to make sacrifices to strengthen those relationships?
If so, what are they?

_____

_____

_____

_____

_____

Chapter 8

THE COURAGE TO LOOK WITHIN

Why do people do the things they do? What causes them to behave the way they do? What motivates them to accomplish or achieve certain things in life? For the answers to these questions and those like them, we really have to look within. Though many people may think they know themselves and others, we cannot see within the soul—where the mind, will, and emotions reside—or what is in the heart. We may get to know others over the course of time in a very intimate way as we mutually share our experiences, hopes, dreams, and even secrets with them. But there is still limited access, for only God can see within the soul.

Sometimes, it really takes courage to truly look within ourselves to see what is really there—the hidden thoughts, desires, and emotions that are tucked away and not dealt with. We may think or feel that most, if not all, areas of our hearts are perfectly fine. But if we really take the time to examine and reflect on the things we've experienced in life, we have to consider how we really feel.

Life is a journey full of discovery and change. As we discover and uncover certain things about ourselves, many times we have to make the adjustments where necessary in order to continue to grow and mature. This continuous growth and development enables and empowers us to be men and women of purpose. Discovering who we truly are liberates us to be free to be the best at what we've been created to do for God, ourselves, and others.

LOOKING WITHIN

In the play *Hamlet*, Shakespeare wrote the prolific statement: "To thine ownself be true." In the play, Polonius gives his son Laertes this advice just as he is about to leave for Paris. He goes on to tell him to be himself. Don't try to be someone you're not. Be real. Oftentimes, when we are not true to ourselves, we end up deceiving ourselves in an attempt to be someone we really aren't. We can get so caught up in the day-to-day interactions with other people and the things going on around us that, if we aren't careful, we end up losing ourselves in the process. But the key to being an authentic individual is having a pure heart and really knowing who you are from the inside out.

We are the sum total of the experiences and influences in our lives. All we have experienced from childhood to the present has helped to shape and mold our personalities and identities. The different people who affected our lives, whether positively or negatively, have all played a part in the person we've become. Having the courage to look at the person within requires us to take a closer look at who we truly are, not the person we want others to think we are.

There are many who look within themselves only to dislike who they see within. However, the realization that we have certain issues that we struggle with cannot be ignored. As we take the time and effort to identify our inner struggles, we can take them to God in prayer and receive the wisdom and guidance necessary to bring about change. The Word is like a mirror. As we look in it, it will show us who we really are. When our thoughts and actions fall in line with the Word of God, we will experience positive result in life. When they don't, we will experience struggles. For our lives to reflect what is in the Word, we must continue to keep the Word in our hearts by reading It on a daily basis. Regardless of what issues we face—past or present, good or bad—we can find the solution in the Word of God.

Looking within may require us to face some really tough issues, but as we expose and uncover them, we allow God to do a work in us. Then the experience becomes a testimony to others of the goodness and faithfulness of God. If we are not real with others, how can we be a witness? We don't have to go around telling all of our business, but we must be willing to be real with others and let them know that we are all dealing with something in our lives. Others will not be drawn to God if they see Christians who are pretenders. People are not eager to put their trust in pretenders because they are focused on perpetuating an illusion. And we cannot trust illusions because they always draw our attention away from what is real.

It is important for us to realize that God wants us to be free in every area of our lives. As we take inventory of the treasure in our hearts, we will discover some truly wonderful and not-so-wonderful things there. But uncovering and discovering them bring enlightenment. As we discover what lies beneath the surface, we begin to understand who we are, and we give others the opportunity to understand us as well.

WHY DO WE DO WHAT WE DO?

Every issue in our lives stems from what is within. This includes why we do the things we do. Whatever is on the inside will eventually be seen on the outside. Whether it's low self-esteem, pride, unforgiveness, appreciation, love, commitment, or some other underlying factors, they will determine our thoughts and our actions. It is within the heart that we can find the true reason or motive behind why we do what we do.

Sometimes we take a lot of baggage into relationships instead of getting free and whole in the presence of God. But once we are free, we are able to freely love and accept love from others. At the beginning of my marriage, I had a hard time dealing with the fact that I was supposed to submit to my husband as the head of our household. As a young child, I saw my mother go through things that I was not willing to let any man have the opportunity to do to me. So every time Creflo was trying to help by giving me suggestions or asking me to do things, I instantly reacted in a negative way. I felt he was trying to control and disrespect me. Over time, I came to realize that I have been blessed with a good husband, and I could not make him suffer for the wrongs of others.

Asking for God's help as I made the decision to study His Word in this area freed me. Being free from baggage allows us to become more compassionate and see things from the perspective of others, even if their perspective is wrong. Most people who act out of insincere motives do so because of the unresolved issues within their hearts. Therefore, we must pray for each other with a sincere heart, realizing that the same God who freed us is able to free them also.

PURE MOTIVES

While man looks at the outer appearance, God looks at our hearts. Many times in life we have to judge our hearts by asking questions like: Why do I do the things I do? Am I going above and beyond my duties at work to simply be noticed or because I am a diligent and dedicated worker? Do I help others to be seen or for what I can get out of the deal, or am I doing it because it honors God? Doing right things for the wrong reasons still doesn't make things right. When we are honest with ourselves and others, we can expect to get the right results.

I remember a few years back when my family came in from out of town to visit our church. I happened to be preaching that Sunday, so I was concerned about what they would think. Instead of preaching what I had studied and was prepared to preach, I decided to preach on something that would be more impressive, in my opinion. During that time, we had two services. As I ministered the sermon that I chose, I stumbled and fumbled from beginning to end. When I left the pulpit, I was drained and, not to mention, quite frazzled. I knew I had made a big mistake. I had to come to the realization that I was not supposed to preach that sermon. As I prayed, I realized I had ignored God's agenda for my own. During the second service, I preached what I had initially planned, and everything went much more smoothly.

While I was doing the right thing by ministering the Word of God, my decision to change the message based on my own selfish reasons, placed me outside of what God had purposed for me to do.

Having motives that are driven by sincere and pure hearts will bring about the will of God for our lives. James 4:3 talks about wrong motives as one of the reasons prayers are not answered. In Matthew 20:20-28 the mother of James and John was worshiping Jesus. While this was a good act, she was not doing it for the right reason. She had a hidden agenda. She was worshiping Him in hopes that this would help to get the result she desired—seats for her sons on each side of Jesus in heaven.

God always looks at our hearts. When we put our faith and trust in Him, we don't have to manipulate, scheme, or plot to obtain the things we desire according to His plan. He will give them to us. And when He gives them to us, nothing or nobody can take it away. True promotion and prosperity—wholeness in every area of our lives—comes from God. He is looking for people He can trust His blessing and favor with. Psalm 24:3-4 AMP says: "Who shall go up into the mountain of the Lord? Or who shall stand in His Holy Place? He who has clean hands and a pure heart." In other words, the condition of our hearts determines our altitude. Success is not determined by what we did, but the reasons behind what was done.

When we accomplish things with clean hands and a pure heart, we receive lasting and rewarding results in life.

GUARD YOUR HEART

When change occurs on the inside of our hearts, it causes a change on the outside. True change will never happen from the outside in. I can remember when I was a little girl, biting into an apple and finding a worm inside. It was really intriguing to me. I wondered how that worm got inside that apple. I later found out that during the summer small fruit flies can be found flying in the apple orchards. These are called apple maggot flies. Each female finds herself a sweet-smelling apple that is ripening, and she lands on it. Using a small, sharp, hollow tube on the underside of her body, the fly stabs a small hole in the fruit. Then she releases her eggs, which slide down that hollow tube into the apple. Soon afterward, the eggs hatch into tiny, white worms, causing the apple to become contaminated.

Likewise, if we are not careful, negative things can penetrate our hearts, causing contamination. As I mentioned earlier, our hearts are gardens. We have to look at what has been planted inside our hearts to determine if anything has taken root there that will taint or contaminate our hearts. Negative influences are all around us. Certain television programs, movies, music, books, and other forms of media are designed to pollute the heart. Therefore, we must be very careful to discern what we feed our souls. The Bible tells us that the pure in heart shall see God. (Matt. 5:8.) When our hearts are pure, we will see God show up on our jobs, in our marriages, in our children, in our finances, and in all other areas of our lives.

As we keep the Word of God in our hearts, the desire for truth, honesty, and integrity grows within and works its way to the outside, producing pure motives. We are instructed in Proverbs 4:23 to diligently guard our hearts. Guarding ourselves against negative talk and negative people helps us to keep our hearts guarded and free from contamination. We may consider certain things that we put into our hearts to be harmless, but we must be careful and diligent to guard it against hidden negative devices that sneak in undetected. When we put the right things in our hearts, we will get the right results in our lives.

THE REAL DEAL

As believers, we will often find that God puts us in situations that will cause us to judge our hearts because we judge ourselves by our own intentions, whereas we judge others by their actions. When our hearts are pure, we do what needs to be done, regardless of what others may say or do. Sometimes our actions may be perceived incorrectly by others, but God looks at the heart, and ultimately, that is what matters most. He is a God who will cause us to always triumph when we follow His agenda.

We never have to compromise our standards or conform to worldly devices to prosper in life. Out of a pure heart comes sincere motives. As true and authentic individuals, with no hidden agenda, we become clear vessels that God can freely use.

Truly looking within causes us to be honest with ourselves about who we are at the very core of our being. When we have the courage to look within, we can honestly answer questions like: What drives my actions? What causes me to behave a certain way? What are my motives?

- *Exploring our innermost thoughts and feelings not only takes courage but can be a painful process as well. However, it is necessary for us to know where we are so that we can reach the destination God has planned for us.*

What are the positive thoughts, motives, and desires that have kept you moving in a positive direction?

_____

_____

_____

_____

_____

_____

What are the negative thoughts, motives, desires, and emotions that have hindered your progress?

_____

_____

_____

_____

What are some ways you can diminish negativity in your life and move forward?

_____

_____

_____

_____

- *There is an old saying that refers to self-confidence as being "comfortable in your own skin." To discover our authenticity, we have to be honest about who we are and be at peace with how God has designed us.*

When you look within, are you comfortable with what you see? Why or why not?

_____

_____

_____

_____

_____

_____

_____

_____

What are some things you can do to be more comfortable with yourself? List positive characteristics, gifts, talents, and skills God has blessed you with.

_____

_____

_____

_____

_____

_____

_____

_____

_____

_____

_____

The Word of God is like a mirror. As we look into it, we can see the reflection of who we really are according to God's principles. How has His Word helped you to see who you are?

_____

_____

_____

_____

_____

How has the Word helped you make positive changes in your life?

_____

_____

_____

_____

_____

• *Most of us can sense when people are being phony. Instead of telling the truth about who they are, they opt to create an illusion to keep others from discovering who they really are.*

What can you do to help others be more open and honest about themselves?

_____

_____

_____

_____

_____

_____

_____

Instead of hiding your flaws, how can you use them to be a blessing to others?

_____

_____

_____

_____

_____

_____

Chapter 9

THE POWER OF FORGIVENESS

There is a quote that says, "Forgiveness is crucial to any life experience because as human beings we will inevitably make mistakes and hurt others." Forgiving others, and even ourselves, is probably one of the hardest things to do because it challenges our emotions and forces us to decide whether we are going to move forward or not. We have all experienced times when we've been mistreated, abused, or hurt in some way. We were then faced with the decision whether or not we would forgive the one who hurt us, or whether we would hold on to what was done to us. Everyone's experience with offense is different, but there is one thing we all have in common: we must forgive in order to progress and move forward in our lives. No matter how we have been wronged, forgiveness is the key that sets us free from the pain of the past.

To forgive someone simply means to pardon them of an offense. Another definition says, "to stop being angry or resentful against." Many people think you have to feel like forgiving before you can actually do it, or they think that negative feelings disappear just because you forgive someone. This is not always the case. Forgiveness is actually a decision. It is something you have to make up in your mind to do on purpose.

You may be wondering why forgiving others is so important. The main reason is because God instructs us to do so, and it is an act of love. In fact, forgiving others ensures that God will forgive us when we miss the mark. Matthew 6:14-15 KJV says, "For if ye forgive men their trespasses, your heavenly Father will also forgive you: But if ye forgive not men their trespasses, neither will your Father forgive your trespasses." There is a direct correlation between your decision to forgive people and the forgiveness God will extend toward you.

There is an account in the Bible of Jesus talking to His disciples about forgiveness. During the discussion, Peter poses an interesting question: "Then Peter came to Jesus and asked, 'Lord, how many times shall I forgive my brother when he sins against me? Up to seven times?' Jesus answered, 'I tell you, not seven times, but seventy-seven times'" (Matt. 18:21,22 NIV). Can you imagine forgiving someone seventy-seven times per offense? This is an extreme example, but I believe God is letting us know how important forgiveness is—so important that He assigned what seems like an unthinkable number to the amount of times we should forgive others.

FORGIVE BY FAITH

When it comes to forgiving others, we often have conditions attached to it. In other words, we are willing to forgive based on the circumstances. Choosing to forgive based on conditions doesn't work because we never really release the person in our hearts. When we try to forgive based on our feelings and emotions, there are many things that can happen to prevent us from ever receiving what it is we are expecting from the other person. Sometimes those who hurt or offend us never come to the realization that they did so, or they may simply choose not to acknowledge it. Clearly, forgiveness cannot be based on the actions of others. If it were, sometimes it would be virtually impossible to forgive.

Choosing to walk in love, regardless of whatever situations and circumstances we face, enables us to forgive. Walking in love is not based on how we feel; it is a decision to love by faith. We walk by faith, not by sight. As we walk by faith, we choose to do the opposite of what feels right—attempting to satisfy our hurt feelings. When we love by faith, it means we love, as well as forgive, in spite of our emotions because it pleases God.

The Bible says, "Love never fails"(1 Cor. 13:8 NIV). This means that no matter what was done to us, if we choose love's route, the outcome will always work out in our favor. If we can't trust anything else, we can know without a shadow of a doubt that handling the situation God's way will produce results. We forgive out of obedience rather than whether it feels good.

Operating in forgiveness is not always easy, especially when you have been deeply hurt or taken advantage of by someone. Creflo and I have had to forgive people for things that, to most people, would seem unforgiveable. People we love and care for, and had even trusted at one time, have ended up hurting us and betraying that trust. Even when it comes to the media, there are assumptions made about our church, and things are said to discredit our character. But we have determined in our minds that we will forgive as an automatic response to offense.

You may feel you've been hurt to such a point that you just can't forgive. It may seem impossible in light of what was done to you. You may have even told yourself you will never be able to forgive what someone did to you. But let me tell you, you can forgive if you believe God's Word.

The Bible talks about how we have the ability to love people the way God does. The very same love with which the Father loves Jesus belongs to us too (John 17:26), and this love has been deposited in our hearts by the Holy Spirit. (Rom. 5:5.) When you accept Jesus into your life, something phenomenal happens—His love for people becomes your love for people. The love of God in you enables you to forgive even the worst act perpetrated against you. The love of God becomes a part of you and empowers you to love those who are unlovable. Forgiveness may seem to be an impossible task, but you have the ability within you to do it. You can forgive anyone for anything at any time. The key is to do it by faith.

An important thing to remember about faith is that it doesn't look at the circumstances and situations before it acts. Neither does it wait for an apology or change of heart on the part of others who hurt us before we forgive. Faith acts now! It empowers us to forgive now, love now, and let go—now.

UNFORGIVENESS CAN HURT YOU

Unforgiveness is a negative emotion that can have a serious effect on our souls and even our physical health. It is like dirt that clogs up the pipeline to your relationship with God and blocks the channels that enable His power to flow into your life. Another way of looking at it is drinking poison, yet hoping the other person will die. We think we are hurting those who hurt us, but we are actually hurting ourselves. It is like we are keeping ourselves chained to those who hurt us while they go on with their lives. It is just not worth it.

When we don't forgive, we also allow bitterness into our hearts and minds, which makes it even more difficult to let go of the past. Bitterness is like a poisonous root that infects us with negativity. The Bible says bitterness defiles us when we allow it to spring up in our lives. (Heb. 12:15.) However, forgiveness is the answer that liberates us from every negative emotion connected to an offense perpetrated against us.

I believe another reason why forgiveness is so vital in the life of a Christian is because it demonstrates the character of God to others, and it allows them to see that our relationship with Him is real. As Christians, we send a message to others by the way we live. As we spend time in God's Word and His presence, we are strengthened and empowered to handle situations that challenge our love walk. Additionally, spending time in His presence and His Word matures and allows us to see situations through His eyes. In today's society, the attitude of forgiveness is not easily seen. We live in a time when the prevailing attitude says "do what feels right," and "an eye for an eye." Having a forgiving attitude that is quick to overlook an offense is not the norm. This is why it speaks so loudly when we choose to respond in love. People can sense something different about us when we walk in forgiveness. And, although they may not acknowledge it or even respond to it, as we continue to make decisions to forgive, regardless of who or what it is, we continue to position ourselves to live authentic and blessed lives.

The other day I was reading an article about a man who was coping with the murder of an immediate family member. In the interview, he was asked how he felt about the killer and how he was dealing with the tragedy. When asked these questions, the man stated that he had forgiven the killer; and he knew that if he didn't, he would always be in torment about what happened. I believe, based on his response, that this man was indeed a Christian, although it was never mentioned. It truly takes the love of God to enable a person to forgive someone who has committed a horrible crime against a loved one.

This man had a revelation of the liberating power of forgiveness, and he made the decision to walk in love. I'm sure it wasn't easy and that his emotions cried out to hate, get revenge, or hold on to what had happened. But none of those things would change the situation or bring his family member back. In the end, all he would be left with would be his memories and the pain he felt inside. But forgiveness has set him on the path to healing and closure. Forgiveness truly brings about healing.

When we choose to forgive, we surrender to the will of God and allow Him to get involved. He can then heal our hurting hearts as we cast our cares on Him, for He truly cares for us. When we simply say that we forgive, that is it. We give all of the hurt and disappointment to Him, trusting Him to restore and release us from the past.

Is there a situation or a person toward whom you are holding unforgiveness? Has bitterness, stemming from the hurt of the past, crept into your heart? If so, I encourage you to examine those areas and take them to God in prayer. He is waiting with open arms to restore and heal what has been damaged. Even if the person you are holding unforgiveness toward is not a part of your life, or even alive, you can still experience the freedom and life-changing power of God's love through forgiveness.

FORGIVING YOURSELF

Sometimes the forgiveness that is needed is not for someone else but for ourselves. Knowing and understanding the power of God's love is what enables us to release the mistakes we have made in life and to move forward.

In order to forgive ourselves, I believe we need to know God can and will forgive us when we confess our faults to Him. First John 1:9 says that He is faithful and just to forgive us of our sins. We are God's beloved! So, when we honestly come to Him and talk with Him about how we have fallen short and ask for His forgiveness, He is quick to forgive.

If God can forgive us, why is it that we have such a hard time forgiving ourselves? Usually, it is because we hold ourselves to such unrealistic standards that when we don't live up to those standards we end up condemning ourselves.

I have learned that setting unrealistic goals or standards only sets us up for disappointment. And although we have desires to fulfill those goals or standards, we cannot be everything to everybody. We have to set boundaries and stick to them. When we've done the best we can do, that is all that is required. I used to start thinking about my day as soon as I got up in the morning, and I was exhausted before noon just thinking about how I was going to get all of those things accomplished! Wearing many hats can cause us to feel obligated and pulled in many different directions. But we must realize that it's okay to forgive ourselves when we can't be all things to all people. God extends His mercy to us every day. With each new day, He gives us a new start with brand new mercy. We only need to accept His love and compassion by faith. This allows us to live free of bondage and to release disappointments.

Through counseling other people, I have noticed that those who have a hard time forgiving others have an even harder time forgiving themselves. This leaves them very little room for error for themselves or others. In fact, not being able to forgive ourselves is probably one of the first areas we need to investigate when we find we just can't let go of unforgiveness. Forgiveness starts with looking within and examining our own deep-rooted heart issues.

Is there anything you're holding on to that you have done and you need to forgive yourself for? If so, say this prayer:

> Heavenly Father, I thank You that there is nothing I can do or say that can separate me from Your love. I come to You now, asking that you forgive me for the times I have missed the mark, specifically _____. I receive your love and forgiveness now. I also forgive myself today for _____, as well as anything I have done to violate another person in thought, word, or deed. I forgive by faith, and I thank You that I am forgiven. In Jesus' name, I pray. Amen.

Forgiving yourself is one of the most liberating things you can do to set yourself and others free from past mistakes. Decide to live each day free of unforgiveness and full of unconditional love.

RELAX, RELATE, RELEASE

A major key to forgiveness is choosing not to rehearse the problem once we have forgiven. We have all found ourselves doing this at times. We find ourselves replaying the incident in our minds over and over again, re-enacting what was said or done, and even picturing what we would do or say to the person if we had the chance. But rehearsing only perpetuates feelings of bitterness and unforgiveness.

Because our thoughts determine our feelings, we have to consciously choose to think the right things about people. Instead of rehearsing what they did to us, we need to dismiss it and let it go. We can take control of our thought lives by thinking about what the Bible says about how to respond to certain situations. Instead of directing negative thoughts and energy toward people, we can choose to surround them with thoughts of love. Even though it may be difficult at first, we can do it by faith. Ask God to help you walk in His love and see people as He does, no matter what they have done. Consider what Jesus suffered at the hands of those who despised Him and encourage yourself with His example of love and forgiveness.

Trying to get even with people who have hurt or disappointed us will hinder our own healing process. When we get caught up in negative emotions, it is tempting to consider ways we can get back at them. But whatever we do, we must choose to diffuse the temptation. We do this by refusing to rehearse the offense in our minds. If we don't nip those negative thoughts in the bud, over time, we will become consumed with what they did to us.

God is completely aware of everything we have been through, but He wants our lives to become living testimonies of His light and love. It is when we choose to forgive, as an act of our will, that we open the door for Him to vindicate us. As we continue to sow seeds of love and pray for those who have hurt us, healing will take place in our own hearts. Love never fails. As we continue to receive His unconditional love for us, we will also continue to spread that love wherever we go. As we do, we receive the liberating power of forgiveness.

To forgive or not forgive, that is the question. Forgiving others is probably one of the hardest things to do because it challenges our emotions and forces us to decide whether we are going to move forward or not. However, it is very critical that we as Christians learn to forgive. It is also very necessary because human beings will make mistakes, and those mistakes can hurt us. Instead of rehearsing the hurt over and over again, we must choose to forgive, so we can heal and move forward.

- *Forgiveness simply means pardoning an offense or choosing to stop being angry or resentful against someone. Many people think they have to feel like forgiving someone before they can actually do it. However, forgiveness is a decision, not a feeling.*

Make a list of people you have forgiven for a past offense.

_____

_____

_____

_____

_____

Make another list of those you have yet to forgive. Pray over the list, and ask God to help you forgive them.

_____

_____

_____

_____

_____

Forgiving others is important because God commanded us to do so. It is an act of love. In addition, forgiving others ensures that God will forgive us when we sin or miss the mark. (Matt. 6:14,15.) Are you willing to make the necessary changes and forgive those you have yet to forgive? If so, make a quality decision to forgive them. If not, why?

_____

_____

_____

_____

- *Sometimes we want to forgive someone with conditions attached to our forgiveness. However, forgiveness cannot be based on the actions of those who have hurt us. We forgive by faith because we love by faith.*

Are there times in your life that you have had to forgive someone by faith? Who were they? How did you do it?

_____

_____

_____

There are times when we have to forgive someone for what may be considered unforgiveable. Have you ever forgiven someone for something you would call unforgiveable? If not, do you think you could? Why or why not?

_____

_____

_____

_____

Unforgiveness is a negative emotion that infects like a poison. It affects both our souls and our physical bodies. In what other ways does unforgiveness hurt us? What are the ways you have seen it hurt others in your life?

_____

_____

_____

_____

_____

How has holding unforgiveness hurt you or hindered your progress?

_____

_____

_____

_____

_____

• *Many times, when we sin or make a mistake, we find it hard to forgive ourselves and release it from our lives. In addition, we tend to set unrealistic expectations for ourselves, and when we fail, we feel condemned. However, we must keep in mind that God is faithful and just to forgive our sins. (1 John 1:9.) And if He can forgive us, we can forgive ourselves.*

Are there sins in your life that you have yet to forgive yourself for? What are they?

_____

_____

_____

_____

Have you asked for God's forgiveness?

_____

_____

_____

_____

Are there mistakes you have made that hold you in condemnation?
What are they?

_____

_____

_____

_____

_____

Have you told God about them in prayer? Why or why not?

_____

_____

_____

_____

_____

Are you holding yourself to unrealistic standards and expectations? Explain.

_____

_____

_____

_____

_____

_____

Chapter 10

LIVING IN AUTHENTICITY

What do people take away with them when they spend time with you? Do they leave encouraged or inspired? Are they able to walk away with some of the answers they were seeking? Are they better off after spending time with you, or do they remain the same? As believers our goal should be to make a difference in the lives of those we meet and know. Our mere presence should be of some benefit to them because we are blessed to be a blessing.

When was the last time you talked to someone about God or took the opportunity to plant seeds in someone's life about accepting Christ? God wants everyone to be saved. That's His agenda. As His ambassadors, we should strive to save the lost. With each new day, we have opportunities to make a difference in someone's life. A simple gesture like eye contact, a smile or a *hello* could be the one thing that makes a difference in someone's day. Kindness will make you stand out from the rest. Those small opportunities could make a huge difference in the life of someone who may need advice or counseling. People are naturally drawn to the light. Is your light shining, or are you blending in with the rest of the world?

There are times when we may feel that we are on a fast track moving forward in life. Our schedules are filled with appointments, board meetings, social gatherings, and other commitments. We get caught up in the commitments and appointments, wishing we could add more hours to the day. We get up early, leave work late, shuttle the kids off to their activities, prepare dinner, eat dinner, go over homework, put the kids to bed, and the list continues. When people ask us how we're doing, many of us have one simple response: "Busy!" Somehow we manage to get most things done, but what are we really achieving?

I have discovered that keeping busy doesn't constitute progress. I can get involved in a lot of the things I'm interested in, and I can work hard, but I want to make a difference in this world. I want my life to matter. When God reviews my account in heaven, I don't want Him to tell me how many hours I was at the office or how many miles I drove each week. I want Him to tell me the number of lives I influenced. I want to hear about the lives that were saved, the people who felt like giving up but were able to overcome and do great things because our paths crossed at some point. I want to make a difference. Don't you?

ONE OF A KIND

God wants to use you to make a mark in this world. Every believer has a pulpit. It may not be a pulpit in a church, but God has given you a pulpit somewhere. It may be your desk at work, a room in your home, or the gym where you work out. The place isn't nearly as important as the numerous opportunities God gives you to touch someone's life in a magnificent way.

I used to minister a lot at the grocery store. When the young men would put my bags in the trunk of my car, I would take the opportunity to minister to them. One day, a young guy pushed a shopping cart up to my car and said, "Wow, ma'am! I like your car. It's so pretty."

I said, "You know what? God gave me this car, and He'll give you one, too, just like He gave this one to me. I love God, and because I love Him, I go to church and read my Bible at home. Do you go to church?"

"No, ma'am," he said. "I work on Sundays, and I really don't go to church."

"That's okay," I assured him. "God still loves you and you can have everything He has for you."

That was it. It was just a small seed planted in the mind of an impressionable young man. I don't know what happened after we met that day, but I just believe that God used that seed to draw him closer. At the right time, I believe that young man will develop a relationship with Christ.

I could have ignored his remark about my car and jumped in the car right away, but I didn't. When we slow down a little, we will discover the opportunities God gives us to minister to others. The fact that I spoke to the young man and carried on a conversation with him meant something. Too often we brush people off, rushing here and there, and we miss the small moments.

People are looking at us, and they are looking to us for encouragement. They want to see the difference our relationship with God is making in our lives. When we react the same as they do while handling problems, they find it hard to understand why they should go through the motions of reading the Bible, going to church, and giving their lives to Christ. But when they see us dealing with some of the same problems they face in a better way, they will want to know more about the God we serve.

Years ago, when I was attending college in Carrolton, Georgia, I heard about a young man who was making a tremendous impact in the lives of the students there. His reputation preceded him, and he had a major influence on the entire campus. College students were getting saved every week, and the new "in" thing was attending Bible study. It was more popular than going to the club or partying. I couldn't believe the impact this guy was having on people. Everywhere I went students were talking about him, the Bible study he taught, and how they really understood his message.

At first, I wasn't interested in the idea because God wasn't on my agenda. To be honest, I was on my way to hell. I didn't know that there was a God. I hated the church, and I didn't want to have anything to do with anything that involved church or God. But my classmates kept talking about this guy, so I said, "I think I might need to go check this out." Little did I know that the man I'd been hearing so much about would change my life forever!

I had met other guys who wanted to be in ministry. But when hard times came or they were tempted, they just kind of fell away. I have to say that the one thing that made me so interested in the guy who was teaching Bible study was how different he was. Talking about Jesus didn't embarrass him, and he wasn't afraid of what people said about him. Right in the middle of all the activities that happen on college campuses, there he was doing what he believed God called him to do. He was willing to be different. That said a lot to me. I had never seen anything like it.

When I went the first time, I expected to see an older gentleman. Even his name sounded like someone older. However, when I walked in and saw this young guy teaching about the Bible, I said, "Wow, this is different."

At the time, none of my family members were born again. By continuing to feed my heart God's Word and attending Bible study regularly, I got saved. I started reading the Bible and going to church. My family just considered me weird. They were saying things like, "What's come over her?" Change had come because of my relationship with Christ. It was the best thing that could have ever happened to me. Later on, as a result of my decision to accept Christ, my parents got saved, my brothers got saved, and even some of my cousins got saved. It was an awesome experience for our family.

Eventually, I entered into a relationship with the young man who taught the Bible study. What attracted me most about him was his willingness to stand up and stand out for what he believed in. It distinguished him from all the rest. Today we are married and have five lovely children. Yes, that man was Creflo Dollar. Just by doing the thing God called him to do, Creflo made a difference in the city, state—and now the world!

TAKING THE CALL SERIOUSLY

Whether you know it or not, we all have the capacity to influence others in some way or another. We do it every day. Our goal should be to make a positive influence in someone's life. There is a tremendous impact that God wants to express through our lives by His goodness and love. To belittle the assignment He has given us would be a shame. We must take our title as Christians seriously. People are not impressed when we carry our Bibles. They want to see the impact the Bible is having in our lives. They want to see the love of God in us. They certainly don't need to be preached to; they've probably experienced that before. To be brutally honest, many people are turned off by Christians because of the hypocrisy, double standards, and criticism sometimes associated with believers.

In one of his letters to the church, Paul expressed how our very lives serve as our letters of recommendation. The characteristics of our personalities represent our credentials as believers. It is in the way we live that people perceive who we are because what is in our hearts comes out through our actions. Yes, people are watching.

You may say, "Nobody's paying attention to me. I just go to work and come home every day." But you'd be surprised. At the very least, your neighbors, coworkers, and family are watching. People who you don't even know are watching you all the time. They can't see God, but they can see you. Think about it. What are they seeing in your life?

God is concerned about the lost. He wants to bring them into reconciliation and develop a relationship with them. God's purpose for giving us influence is intentional. It's not to be used just for our own purposes. He has given us influence so that we can use it to build His kingdom. We can be a part of His great plan when we do our part, operating in the influence that comes from Him.

The word *influence* is defined as "the act or power of producing an effect without any apparent exertion." This is what happens to others when they are around you. You probably work at a job where there are people who aren't saved. And you may have been praying to the Lord to deliver you from that job because of some of the challenges you face in the environment. But consider this: since you are there at this time, could it be that He has a plan? I'm sure you could find a rewarding job someplace else, but why does God have you at this place at this time? Perhaps it is because He wants you to make a positive impact in the lives of the people you work with. Are they able to tell whether you are a Christian? Do you take your role as Christian more seriously than you take your official job title? I'm not saying you should go to work with Christian music blasting or read your Bible at your desk. No, you were hired to do a particular job, and you would dishonor God if you didn't do your job properly. What I am asking is whether you are allowing your light to shine— not through a bumper sticker on your car or the cross you wear around your neck but in the way that you carry yourself.

I am reminded of a story I heard about a woman who was stopped by a police officer one day. She was at a red light. When the light turned green, the man in front of her just sat there. Obviously she was upset and in a hurry, so she began honking the horn, cursing and yelling at him to move out of the way. By the time he finally moved, the light was yellow, so she had to sit through the next light. She was still cursing and throwing up her hands even after the man left. While she was waiting, an officer tapped on the window and asked her to step out of the car. She responded, "For what?"

The officer said, "I just need you to step out of the car, ma'am."

When she got out, he handcuffed her, put her in the patrol car, and took her downtown to the police station. After sitting there for awhile, the officer came back and acknowledged that he had made a mistake. The woman replied, "Why did you arrest me, officer?"

He answered, "When I pulled up and read the various bumper stickers on your car like "Honk if you love Jesus," "I'm on my way to heaven," and "Praise the Lord," and then saw how you were carrying on at the light, I instinctively thought you had stolen the car. I just figured there was no way you could be a Christian."

The moral of the story is that people don't judge us based on what we wear or what we tell them. They base their decisions on what we say and do. This lady's car had Christian bumper stickers all over it. But the person the officer saw didn't represent the character of a Christian at all. Our actions influence those who see us.

What children see at home and what they see in public can sometimes pose a problem for children who are raised by Christians, even those raised by pastors. Children are confused by what they see their parents do at church and around other Christians versus what they see them do elsewhere. Often the two don't match, and there is an extreme imbalance in the authentic personality and the masked personality.

This parallels with what Peter was referring to in 1 Peter 3:1-2 when he talked about the unsaved spouse being won over by the saved spouse's lifestyle. The words and actions carried out by the saved spouse have the power to positively influence the one who is not saved. If you have an unsaved spouse or unsaved children, don't preach to them. Don't put a salvation tract on the pillow or pour anointing oil all over the door or headboard. That won't change anything. It can, however, frustrate the situation and sour the relationship. Your loved ones want to see God in you. If you're mean and hateful, always yelling and neglecting to spend time with them, they are not going to be inclined to desire a relationship with God. Instead, just live your life. Love them into the things of God. Be a good example because you have the greatest influence over them.

INFLUENCE VS. CONTROL

To be clear, influence is not control. Some people mistakenly believe they have the authority to use their influence in a negative way. They do not. Being self-centered does not influence people in a positive way. People do not want to be around someone who's always trying to manipulate or take advantage of them. They are more susceptible to those they can trust. If we're not walking in love with those around us, our influence will not bring about the positive results we should desire to have.

There is a big difference between having a positive influence on someone and having control over them. Nobody wants to be controlled. Control is deadly. It is a deadly enemy to relationships. A controlling spirit destroys careers and, ultimately, lives, if it is not careful.

No one wants a controlling boss—someone who is constantly looking over his or her shoulder. A boss like this can only get so much productivity. Sure, people will work hard and do the things expected of them when they're being watched like a hawk, but as soon as the hawk leaves the room, it's back to business as usual. In most cases, employees who have a controlling boss lack respect for them. It is nearly impossible for someone to support the mission or vision of someone who is controlling. People will do certain things for a while but there will be no true allegiance, and they will ultimately go someplace else where they are treated fairly and are appreciated.

When my children were younger, it was very easy to control what they watched on television, listened to on the radio, who they talked to on the phone, and where they went because they were with me most of the time. But as they got older, I didn't have those same advantages. I could only pray that the influence I made when they were younger would carry over into their lives as teens and young adults.

WORDS IMPACT OUR INFLUENCE

One day, we will have to give an account to God for every word we say. It is therefore wise that we choose them carefully. If we want to have a positive influence in people's lives, we have to avoid opportunities to gossip, be critical, and complain. Just as a person can affect the atmosphere around them in a positive manner, they can also contribute to a negative atmosphere.

Our choice of words has a lot to do with the type of life we live. Words also affect our overall productivity. When we easily find fault in others and are critical of them, we reap the results of our decisions. That's why the children of Israel stayed in the wilderness for forty years. They complained about everything! "Why did God bring us out here to die? What are we going to eat? We should have stayed in slavery." Despite all that God had done for them (even as they murmured and complained) they didn't acknowledge His provision. And when they did recognize God's miraculous provision, they failed to say so. But the minute they felt afraid or abandoned, they let the faucet flow. As a result, their words affected their blessings and delayed their progress.

We must be accountable for the words we speak. To be accountable means "to be liable, to provide explanation or justification." Each of us is accountable to God for the things we say. In clearer terms, on the day of judgment, we will have to explain or justify why we said what we said. Words define the essence of our being.

Words are also spiritual containers. They have the power to define and redefine reality. The power we activate when we speak is far beyond anything we can perceive. It is like putting a debit card into an ATM to make a transfer from one account to another. Depending on how the money is distributed, we either create a positive or negative balance. That is exactly what we do when we speak: we either make a transfer toward achieving positive or negative results in our lives.

Life and death are in the power of the words we speak. (Prov. 18:21.) Life equals blessings, and death equals curses. However, God is so gracious. He gives us the ability to choose. In His Word, He gives us a hint as to which we should choose. You guessed it: choose life!

THE BLESSING OF INFLUENCE

Abraham's faith made a tremendous impact in the lives of his family and even in our lives today. One of the reasons why God chose Abraham was because of the influence he had in the lives of others. Genesis 12:2 AMP reads, "And I will make of you a great nation, and I will bless you [with abundant increase of favors] and make your name famous and distinguished, and you will be a blessing [dispensing good to others]."

The blessing is an empowerment from God to do supernatural things. In other words, when you have the blessing on your life, you have God's ability working through you to get the job done. He puts His super on your natural, and together the supernatural is accomplished. God also promised to give Abraham great influence by making his name well-known and giving him an abundance of resources to bless others. He wants to do the same in our lives.

In this passage, God promises to make Abraham a great nation. *How can He do that?* you may be wondering. The actual interpretation of that term is an indication that Abraham would have significant authority and influence. Because Abraham allowed God to use him, his impact was far greater than it would have been without God's involvement in his life.

In verse three God goes on to say, "And I will bless those who bless you [who confer prosperity or happiness upon you] and curse him who curses or uses insolent language toward you; in you will all the families and kindred of the earth be blessed [and by you they will bless themselves]." As believers, that's what we've been called to do—dispense good to others.

The same blessings that God gave to Abraham in this covenant are the same blessings available to us today. A covenant is "an agreement formed between two parties that cannot be broken or annulled." Every one of God's promises are true. In fact, I want you to go back and read verse two again. And every time you see the word *you* say your name. This will make it more personal:

And I will make of [insert your name] a great nation, and I will bless [insert your name] [with abundant increase of favors] and make [insert your name]'s name famous and distinguished, and [insert your name] will be a blessing [dispensing good to others].

The blessing causes prosperity: it causes wealth to flow in our lives. It contains every anointing from God. So when we operate in the blessing, we are able to reach people and reconcile them to God through our influence. Part of that blessing is to have influence in reaching people and leading them to God. The blessing ultimately flows from generation to generation.

God has distinguished us as the salt of the earth. (Matt. 5:13.) He wants us to make an impact in the world. Salt is no good in its container, but when it is sprinkled on french fries, it just changes the whole taste. Likewise, when we make contact with others and impact their lives for the better, the world becomes a better place. It can happen one person at a time. You touch a person then they touch another and before you know it, we've got the place covered!

This same ripple effect is how Jesus influenced the lives of millions. Every time He performed a miracle, healed someone, or touched a life in some way, the word spread like wildfire. No one has had a greater influence on history than Jesus. Think of the impact He had on the fishermen. Because they listened to His advice, their nets overflowed with an abundance of fish. As a result, the fishermen left their jobs and became Jesus' followers. When the Samaritan woman met Him at the well, He told her things about her life that only He could know. This influenced her to run and tell everyone! When the people in town heard her story, souls were won to Christ. The Bible says that many more believed because of her testimony. When Jesus healed the man with the crippled hand, people were amazed. As a result, many gave their lives to Him.

THE DISCIPLES' INFLUENCE

One day Peter and John were going into the temple to pray. A man who had been unable to walk since birth asked them to give him money.

> Then Peter said, "Silver or gold I do not have, but what I have I give you. In the name of Jesus Christ of Nazareth, walk." Taking him by the right hand, he helped him up, and instantly the man's feet and ankles became strong. He jumped to his feet and began to walk. Then he went with them into the temple courts, walking and jumping, and praising God. When all the people saw him walking and praising God, they recognized him as the same man who used to sit begging at the temple gate called Beautiful, and they were filled with wonder and amazement at what had happened to him.
>
> Acts 3:6-10 NIV

Peter and John were just going about their day when this opportunity came. This was one of those small moments that happen in life. Had the disciples ignored the man's request for money, this miracle may not have happened. The man was expecting to receive money, but he received much more. He was completely healed!

A multitude began to gather, and the Scripture says the people were amazed. They honestly believed that Peter and John healed the crippled man. When the disciples heard this, they responded by letting them know that it was by Christ's power that the man had been healed. Because Peter and John believed in Christ and had been in relationship with Him, the power of the Almighty worked through them. In other words, God was able to use them to carry out His plan of healing for this man. When we stay in God's presence, His power is available to us as well.

Rather than taking the credit themselves, Peter and John redirected their attention to Jesus and took advantage of the opportunity to minister to the people. The priests and the captain came up as Peter and John were ministering, and they were greatly disturbed because the men were professing Jesus and the power of His resurrection. They were so bothered by the idea that they put the two men in jail. Even then, their influence carried over, and the Bible records that many believed that day. In fact, more than 5,000 people were blessed by the Word of God. Now that's influence. These two men paid attention to the opportunity they had been given and, as a result, thousands were influenced by their boldness and courage.

It's time that we take a bold stand for Christ, just as Peter and John did. So many people are taking a stand for what they believe these days, and people believe in all kinds of things—things that have no power or real significance. But we believe in the all-powerful, everlasting Savior, Jesus Christ!

After the men had taken Peter and John into custody, they began to discuss among themselves what they would do. They admitted that they could not question, deny, or say anything against what the disciples had done because they all knew that the man had been crippled since birth. Now there he was, standing right before them—healed. I just love it when God does something so miraculous that it is undeniable, even to the naysayers. This passage is so powerful. Here is an account of what happened after the disciples were arrested:

> "What are we going to do with these men?" they asked. "Everybody living in Jerusalem knows they have done an outstanding miracle, and we cannot deny it. But to stop this thing from spreading any further among the people, we must warn these men to speak no longer to anyone in this name."
>
> Then they called them in again and commanded them not to speak or teach at all in the name of Jesus. But Peter and John replied, "Judge for yourselves whether it is right in God's sight to obey you rather than God. For we cannot help speaking about what we have seen and heard."
>
> After further threats they let them go. They could not decide how to punish them, because all the people were praising God for what had happened.
>
> Acts 4:16-21 NIV

Isn't that amazing? They couldn't find fault in Peter and John's actions, and they realized the magnitude of their influence in the city. In fact, they attested that "everybody living in Jerusalem" knew about the miracle and had been positively influenced by it. They recognized that Peter and John were not educated men and were only able to perform this miracle because they had been with Jesus. The proof was in the pudding—a notable miracle had taken place. And they were forced to let the disciples go free.

In your own life, you have to begin doing notable things. You may be saying, "Well, I only have the ability to influence one or two people. I'm just a housewife; all I do is feed the baby and change diapers all day." That's fine. Just remain open to God. Let Him use you. Seize the small moments and take advantage of them. You don't know whose diaper you're changing. The Sunday school teacher who ministered to Billy Graham as a child had no idea that he would grow up and impact the lives of millions. Just do what you can do. Let God put His super on your natural. He can multiply your effort in ways you could never imagine.

PROSPERITY HAS INFLUENCE

Money and wealth have great influence. If we conduct a word study on the word *wealth*, we will find that it is not just limited to money; it also refers to being "resourceful." It is having goods, services, and abilities. To be as influential as God would have us to be, we must be givers and not takers. We are blessed to be a blessing to others. We don't possess the things we have just for our own benefit. No. God wants to use our resourcefulness to strengthen others.

In biblical times, there lived a great man who was also blessed with great wealth. God was impressed with this man because when He asked the man what he wanted, the man, in turn, asked God for wisdom and an understanding heart. Wow! What a prayer and what integrity. Many people would have asked God for a house, a car, and money. In fact, people ask Him for those very things every single day. But not this man. He stood out in God's mind as someone who could be used because his priorities were in order. God had given him an impressive position. Rather than seeking wealth, he wanted to understand the heart of the people he oversaw and exercise wisdom in his daily affairs. This man was King Solomon. And in him, God was well pleased.

No king living before or after Solomon has been able to exceed his wealth. The Queen of Sheba heard of Solomon's fame, his great wealth, and his relationship with God. She wanted to see firsthand all that she had heard and test him with a few hard questions. So she set out to visit him. She arrived bearing gifts for him that included spices and large quantities of gold and precious stones. When she stepped foot in the home he had built, she was amazed by what she saw. The place was more beautiful than anything she'd ever seen. Solomon's servants were happy, prosperous, and well-dressed. He was blessed to be a blessing. He didn't keep the wealth to himself. Even Solomon's help was well-off.

When the queen saw King Solomon, however, she was overwhelmed by his presence and good looks. In fact, she fainted. When she finally awakened, she began drilling him with all sorts of questions. He answered every one and held no secrets. His integrity further impressed the queen. She admitted that everything she had heard was true, in fact, more true than she had heard. The queen saw the influence in Solomon's life, and after spending time with him, her life was forever changed! Solomon's faith in God and the rewards of his honesty and faithfulness were undeniable.

Every believer has influence. Our lives have influence. We are the salt of the earth and the light of the world. Galatians 6:10 encourages us to do good to all people when we are given the opportunity. Here are a few tools that you can use to become a greater influence in the lives of others:

Be the manifested Word.

Let's be a demonstration of the Word of God in action. Let's be love in action. Let's be compassion in action. We have to conceive God's Word by planting it in our hearts, meditating on it, and speaking it. Allow it to germinate on the inside so that it can bring forth the manifestation of God's goodness.

Demonstrate love and compassion.

We can't be selfish and expect to make a positive influence in the lives of people. We have to be compassionate and show evidence of God's love. It should be our goal to do whatever we can to be a blessing to others and to help them without reservation or request.

Give.

We must be willing to give freely of not just our money but also our time, talents, and abilities. To be truly influential as God would have us to be, we have to be givers, not takers. Ecclesiastes 9:15-16 reminds us that no one remembers a poor man. Granted, you can have a certain amount of influence in poverty, but you can have a lot more with wealth.

Make contact with the world.

We can't be afraid to reach out to people. There are many ways to make an impact in the world through giving, volunteering, and spending time with people. Start searching for new ways to make an impact in the lives of others. Be committed, and give it your all.

Fulfill God's purpose for your life.

Make God's will for your life a priority. Don't postpone it or decide that you will do it after you've done all the things you want to do. Now is the time to set things right in your life. Ask God what it is that He would be pleased with you doing right now, and begin doing it. Don't delay!

Be stable.

We must display some form of stability and consistency in our lives to influence others in a positive way. Whatever you do, decide that you will do it for the long haul. Don't be in today and out tomorrow. Be committed. That's how you make an impact in the lives of people.

When people spend time with you, make sure you leave a good and lasting impression. It's time for believers to make a mark in this world by being a positive influence in the lives of others. I'm sure there are things in your heart that you've wanted to do for years, but you haven't gotten around to them yet. Make a list and start with one. Maybe you want to volunteer at a local shelter, help feed the hungry on weekends, or minister door-to-door and lead people to Christ. Whatever it is, God has placed the desire in you, and He will support you every step of the way. Now is the time to increase your influence and make a difference in the world.

Living an authentic lifestyle requires that we live a life that blesses others. As we live our lives by the Word of God, we demonstrate the love and compassion for others that mark us as authentic Christians and make a positive impact on the lives of those around us.

- *People are looking at us, and they are looking to us for encouragement. Our goal should be to become a positive influence in the lives of others. People are not impressed when we carry our Bibles. They want to see the impact the Bible is having in our lives. They want to see the love of God in us. The characteristics of our personality are a representation of our credentials as believers.*

In what ways do you make a positive impact in the lives of others?

_____

_____

_____

_____

_____

_____

_____

_____

_____

_____

When you choose to be a blessing in the lives of others, what is your motivation?

_____

_____

_____

_____

What are some of the most effective ways that you can minister to others throughout your day?

_____

_____

_____

_____

_____

_____

- *Our choice of words has a lot to do with the type of life we live. Words also affect our overall productivity. Words are spiritual containers. They hold our future. We create our future by the words we speak. Therefore, we must speak faith-filled, positive words in order to expect things to go well in our lives. Each of us is accountable to God for the things we say.*

What kinds of words are you speaking on a daily basis?

_____

_____

_____

_____

_____

_____

_____

Judging by your words, would others consider you to have a positive or negative outlook on life?

_____

_____

_____

_____

In what ways can we ensure that we speak only positive, faith-filled words in our lives and in the lives of others?

_____

_____

_____

_____

_____

Reflect on the last time you were concerned or uncertain about a particular matter in your life. What were you speaking about that situation?

_____

_____

_____

_____

_____

How did those words affect the outcome?

_____

_____

_____

_____

_____

ABOUT THE AUTHOR

Taffi Dollar and her husband, Creflo Dollar, are the pastors of World Changers Church International in College Park, Georgia, which currently has over 30,000 members. The couple also pastor World Changers Church-New York, where more than 6,000 worshipers gather weekly, and also have over numerous satellite churches across the country.

Taffi Dollar is the president and CEO of Arrow Records, overseer of the women's fellowship, and the founder of Prestige ministry— an outreach ministry for women in the adult entertainment industry.

Dollar ministers throughout the country, and she can be seen worldwide on the *Changing Your World* television broadcast. She lives in Atlanta, Georgia, with her husband and five children.

PRAYER OF SALVATION

God loves you—no matter who you are, no matter what your past. God loves you so much that He gave His one and only begotten Son for you. The Bible tells us that "...whoever believes in him shall not perish but have eternal life" (John 3:16 NIV). Jesus laid down His life and rose again so we could spend eternity with Him in heaven and experience His absolute best on earth. If you would like to receive Jesus into your life, say the following prayer out loud and mean it from your heart.

Heavenly Father, I come to You admitting that I am a sinner. Right now, I choose to turn away from sin, and I ask You to cleanse me of all unrighteousness. I believe that Your Son, Jesus, died on the cross to take away my sins. I also believe that He rose again from the dead so that I might be forgiven of my sins and made righteous through faith in Him. I call upon the name of Jesus Christ to be the Savior and Lord of my life. Jesus, I choose to follow You and ask that You fill me with the power of the Holy Spirit. I declare that right now I am a child of God. I am free from sin and full of the righteousness of God. I am saved in Jesus' name. Amen.

If you prayed this prayer to receive Jesus Christ as your Savior for the first time, please contact us on the Web at **harrisonhouse.com** to receive a free book.

Or you may write to us at

Harrison House

P.O. Box 35035

Tulsa, OK 74153

Experience the Beauty of a Balanced Life!

If you've enjoyed *Authentic: Dare to Be Real!*, you'll love Taffi Dollar's *Your Spiritual Makeover*, now available in paperback! *Your Spiritual Makeover* gives you spiritual and practical methods for ordering and organizing your time. Filled with easy ways to put God first in a busy lifestyle, this interactive and inspiring book will help you find the time you need with God and help you to put all those little details in order for a fulfilled and joyful life—spirit, soul, and body! Available at bookstores everywhere or visit www. harrisonhouse.com.

Fast. Easy. Convenient.

For the latest Harrison House product information and author news, look no further than your computer. All the details on our powerful, life-changing products are just a click away. New releases, E-mail subscriptions, testimonies, monthly specials—find it all in one place. Visit harrisonhouse.com today!

harrisonhouse

THE HARRISON HOUSE VISION

Proclaiming the truth and the power

Of the Gospel of Jesus Christ

With excellence;

Challenging Christians to

Live victoriously,

Grow spiritually,

Know God intimately.